An interesting
with fine ones and
in advances.

Corbyn
and Trident
Labour's continuing controversy

Carol Turner

Published in 2016 by Public Reading Rooms
Visit our website at www.prruk.org
© 2016 Carol Turner
ISBN 978-0-9955352-1-3

Carol Turner is a long-time peace and anti-war campaigner, and a member of the Labour Party. She's a member of the Campaign for Nuclear Disarmament's National Council and chair of London Region CND. Carol has been active in Labour CND since the 1980s, and its national secretary from 1988-2007. She is currently a vice-chair of Labour CND, and also a member of the Stop the War Coalition's Steering Committee.

A foreign policy advisor to British parliamentarians for over 15 years, Carol has worked as a university lecturer and is now an independent researcher and occasional broadcaster on nuclear weapons and Middle East conflicts. She holds a degree in International Politics and a masters degree in Social Research.

To Walter, an example for us all

'They make a desert and call it peace'
Tacitus, 98 AD

Contents

Preface

I WANT to start with a reminder of what this narrative is *really* about, which is so much more than a debate in one of Britain's political parties. The epigraph you've glanced at as you turned the pages is a quotation from *Agricola* by the Roman historian Tacitus, written around 98 AD. 'They make a desert and call it peace' always makes me think of those photos of Japan after the atomic bombs were dropped – not just the devastated landscapes, the empty eyes of the victims as well and the testimonies of the Hibakusha, the survivors. Some of them were still around and sharing their stories when I visited Hiroshima and Nagasaki this August to commemorate the 71st anniversary of the United States' bombing of those cities in 1945.

When I looked it up, this still-remembered phrase of a long-dead historian, I found that a more accurate translation would be: 'To robbery, slaughter, plunder, they give the lying name of empire; they make a solitude and call it peace'. I learned it's a description of the Battle of Mons Graupius which took place in northern Scotland around 83 or 84 AD, and that it's part of a speech which Tacitus attributes to Calgacus, a Caledonian chieftain rousing his troops to fight by describing the 'terrible Romans from whose oppression escape is vainly sought'. It seemed all the more appropriate to me, because Britain's nuclear weapons operate out of the Faslane naval base on the Clyde.

On closer inspection it transpires that the majority of scholars believe the speech, and perhaps even the speaker, to be a figment of Tacitus's imagination. A nice wee tale nonethe-less, with a certain relevance too, bearing in mind that Labour's Trident controversy is also littered with fictions. They are the fictions that the champions of the British bomb would have us believe: that nuclear weapons are a 'deterrent', that Trident is independent, and that we need our own bomb to keep the Rus-sians (and the North Koreans) off our doorstep. From Ernie Bevin to the New Labourites, I've never come across a single atomic warrior who doesn't claim to find Trident as loathsome as I do, and who isn't as eager as me to get rid of it...just as soon as they've got rid of theirs. Until then, of course, we must have a bomb of our own and drape it with the union jack.

The idea that became this book was prompted by Tony Blair's announcement that he wanted to replace Trident. I re-member the general election of 1983, and the debate that fol-lowed Labour's defeat. Nuclear disarmament lost Labour the election, it was claimed, the party's manifesto was the longest suicide note in history. This is a great deception – perpetrat-ed by the likes of Denis Healey and Jim Callaghan who spent the election denouncing nuclear disarmament – and willingly spread by Labour's opponents. (Sound familiar?) These atomic warriors operated on the principle that if you repeat something often enough the idea sticks. And it did. No sooner did Blair announce his next 'modernisation', the British bomb, than the same argument popped up again. It wasn't true, and I wanted to set the record straight.

———————

CORBYN AND TRIDENT began as a project supported by NET, the Nuclear Education Trust, which helped fund research on the evo-lution of Labour's nuclear weapons policy, the interviews with some of those involved, and the archiving of a Labour CND paper mountain that had been built in my back room. The manuscript derives from all of these. So my first thanks are due to NET for believing the project was worthwhile. And thanks too to Mary

Brennan, a CND vice chair in the 1990s, who began the first Labour CND archive when confined to bed with a long illness.

Naive as I was, I imagined a few publishing houses might vie for the manuscript. Not a bit of it. Even the more radical publishers told me 'bomb books don't sell'. (Thank you reader for helping to prove them wrong.) An offer I did have came from one of the biggest international publishers around. They were prepared to take it on if I included all sorts of extra stuff that would sell in their North American and European markets; if so, they would publish the 'monograph' (that's what they call pot-boilers by obscure academics) in hardback at £60 or £70 a pop. My motivation has always been to create a sort of manual for activists. I didn't want to offer a dissociative commentary from the wings, so why put all that work into something which would gather dust on the shelves of a few dozen university libraries? I didn't sign the contract.

So my next thanks are to Public Reading Rooms for agreeing to publish this book. The first drafts were made before Jeremy Corbyn was even a twinkle in your average Labour Party member's eye. So needless to say, it's taken on quite a different character en route to publication. Its final form is a polemic, as powerful an argument as I can make for one point of view in a live and on-going debate. Academic references are stripped to the minimum, as are some of academe's other conventions like tons of footnotes and engaging at length with works by other authors.

I believe the style is merited. The polemicists on the other side of the debate are able to count the majority of the British establishment and the massed ranks of the media among their supporters – not because their arguments carry more force, but because they chime with the vested interests of an ancien régime prepared to spend billions on a weapons system that doesn't protect us from the real security threats we're facing: terrorism, cyber attack, climate change, health pandemics, people trafficking and other forms of modern slavery.

The research behind the book is no less rigorous for the

style it adopts. If you're interested in following through on the details – and I urge you to do so – there'll be a web page up and running by the end of this year containing a lot of the fully referenced material that didn't make it into these chapters. You'll find it via the Public Reading Rooms website.

———

THE BOOK begins and ends with the Labour Party as it is today. Chapter 1 takes a quick look at the new state of affairs that started with Jeremy Corbyn's campaign to become leader, and the relationship between the Corbyn leadership and nuclear disarmament. Chapters 2 to 5 describe three periods in the post-war history of the Labour Party – the Attlee government's decision to build the bomb in the 1940s; Labour's response to US cruise missiles coming to Britain in the 1980s, which sparked widespread fears of a nuclear war in Europe; and the contemporary debate about replacing Trident. Chapter 6 draws a few parallels and contrasts between the three periods, and looks briefly to the future.

The manuscript goes to the publishers as Labour's 2016 annual conference concludes. The results of the leadership challenge have been announced. Corbyn has done a little better even the second time round, with 61.8% of the vote and a majority among members, supporters, and affiliates. This hasn't stopped the attacks from the New Labour rump who have led the charge against Corbyn since before September 2015 – though their format might change, at least for a while. And it appears that Labour will not be continuing the much-disrupted review of its defence policy at present. So any comments as to what the coming months and years might hold for Corbyn and Labour's nuclear disarmament policies are of necessity highly tentative.

———

THE INTERVIEWS are important in giving the reader a behind-the-scenes feel for the topic. Thank you to all the participants. The interviews are described in a bit more detail at the end of the book. They took place in October and November 2013, when the Labour Party was led by Ed Miliband – before the 2015 general election, before Corbyn became leader, and before the 2016 Trident vote.

The extracts I've included are inset within the text, to identify them. They are only minimally edited to remove the occasional repetition or pause (errr, ahh, y'know). Needless to say, agreeing to be interviewed doesn't mean the participants agree with my views. The opinions expressed in the book are mine, not theirs. By the same token, repeating what they told me doesn't imply I agree with them, only that I believe what they're saying is representative of a particular experience or point of view.

———

THANKS to lots of unnamed people who've had an input into what I've written, consciously or not. That includes my colleagues in Labour CND and the many members and supporters I've met in the last year during the dozens of Trident debates we've participated in. Particular thanks also go to Kate Hudson, Andrew Murray, and Marjorie Thompson who've read some or all of the various chapter drafts at one time or another; and to Alice Mahon with whom I discussed the project – at length and often – and whose brains I picked for inspiration, memories and contacts. The same stricture about my views and theirs also applies. Thanks to Cynthia Cockburn who was really helpful as my liaison with NET, in the practical search for publishers and in urging me on when I couldn't find one. And last but not least, a very big thank you to Walter Wolfgang, for his ready fund of knowledge about Labour's post-war years and his good-humoured persistence that's kept the project alive and the author on track.

CAROL TURNER
London, September 2016

CHAPTER 1
The Corbyn phenomenon examined

You don't need a book to tell you something different's going on in British politics today. We're living through unusual times, and witnessing some unexpected responses to the big economic and social questions. Consider for a moment: the success of the Scottish National Party, up from six seats in the 2010 general election to 56 out of 59 Scottish seats in 2015; the rise of UKIP, its role in the European Union referendum and how it's brought racism and xenophobia back into the mainstream; or the Brexit result of the EU referendum in June 2016 which left Britain reeling. And last – but by no means the least important – the election of Jeremy Corbyn and the resurgence of Labour's left wing. A year on, both he and his supporters have not only held out but grown, despite daily hostility from the media.

Unanticipated as they were, these events are not as surprising as they might first appear. We have experienced their forerunners – in the response to Tony Blair's war on Iraq, when the Occupy movement protested the greed and corruption of the City of London, in the enduring public revulsion over MPs' expenses scandals, and in the growth of an anti-austerity movement. Nor are such events confined to a small island off mainland Europe, though their particular expression is distinctive to Britain. The rise of Syriza in Greece and Podemos in Spain, the anti-immigrant protests in France, Italy, Germany, Poland, and the less-reported examples of anti-government, anti-corruption demonstrations in Hungary, Bulgaria, Romania, Moldova are all reflexions of a new mood sweeping Europe and beyond. In North America too, the rise of Bernie Sanders and Donald Trump, and the on-going scepticism over Hillary Clinton, as well the militant fightback of black Americans against police racism and violence are manifestations of our changing times; as were the popular uprisings in the Middle East and north Africa.

Society is polarising, driven by the growing gap between rich and poor, countries as well as people. None of us knows where these politicisations will lead. They are the context in which the rise of Corbyn in Britain takes place.

POPULARITY

When Ed Miliband stepped down as Labour leader after the party's defeat in the 2015 general election, Jeremy Corbyn ran as the outsider candidate, a token leftie with no hope of victory... or so we all thought. Corbyn had difficulty scraping up enough nominations to stand. He reached the minimum threshold, 35 MPs, just two minutes before nominations closed at noon on 15 June according to the BBC, and only with the help of parliamentary colleagues like Margaret Beckett and Frank Field who did not back him but agreed to widen the choice of candidates. When the leadership contenders were announced, Corbyn told the press: 'I will take part in that debate and hope that at the end of it the Labour Party emerges stronger and more resolute in opposing the principles behind austerity and impoverishment of the poorest in Britain.' Prophetic or what?

As the weeks passed it became clear that Corbyn was attracting support well beyond what anyone anticipated. An early indication came at the end of July. When supporting nominations closed, Corbyn topped the Constituency Labour Party poll with 152 CLPs compared to Andy Burnham's 111 and Yvette Cooper's 109. With only 18 supporting CLPs, Liz Kendall had now become the no-hope candidate. Corbyn was also endorsed by two of the big three unions, Unite and Unison. Corbyn's opponents were beginning to worry. John McTernan, a Progress whipper-in, described MPs who'd lent Corbyn their nomination as 'morons'. Beckett felt moved to point out: 'At no point did I intend to vote for Jeremy myself – nice as he is – nor advise anyone else to do it.' In response to media questions Corbyn commented only that it was 'a bit premature' to talk about him winning.

By mid-August 2015 an even plainer picture emerged. Labour had to extend the deadline for registering to vote in the leadership election by three hours because demand was so heavy the party website crashed. The Labour right was seriously worried that the new election system, modelled on US primaries, was not working out in their favour. A YouGov poll showed striking majorities for Corbyn among trade union affiliates and registered supporters, and close on 50% support among individual party members. The *Mirror* announced: 'Corbyn could win by a knockout under new voting procedure'.

When the results were declared at a Labour Party special conference on 12 September, the YouGov survey proved pretty accurate. Turnout was high at 76.3%. Corbyn was elected in the first round with 59. 5% of first preferences – 49.6% among individual members, 57.6% among affiliated supporters, and 83.8% among registered supporters. The number of people who voted for Corbyn, 251,417, came to two-thirds more than the entire membership of the Conservative Party. The results of the leadership contest also revealed how big a gap existed between the Parliamentary Labour Party and Labour members and supporters in the country. The PLP's backing for Burnham and Cooper never materialised among the members or affiliates. Neither achieved even one in five of the votes cast; Kendall managed less than one in 20.

A long-time backbencher, a serial whip-breaker, a man of conviction was now leading the Labour Party. Corbyn represented a real alternative to the Westminster establishment which was increasingly out of touch with public opinion. Young people recognised it and were signing up to Labour in their tens of thousands. Thousands more ex-members were rejoining who'd dropped out in the New Labour years, disheartened by the government's failure to break with neo-liberal economics and incensed by the Labour government's support for war on Iraq.

Corbyn has proved to be a membership magnet. In the 24 hours following his election 14,500 more new members signed up to the Labour Party. The announcement in 2016 of a formal challenge to his leadership saw 184,000 more supporters register to vote in under a week – despite a massive hike in the supporters fee from £3 to £25. At the end of July 2016 Labour Party membership had more than doubled in a year, to 515,000. The party is bigger now than ever before in its history.

The challenge to Corbyn's leadership has revealed a considerable growth in his popularity inside the party. When the deadline for supporting nominations from constituencies and affiliates was reached, he had the backing of 285 CLPs – more than double the 133 local parties that backed him in 2015. He also had supporting nominations from Young Labour's National Committee and eight of the 15 affiliated unions – ASLEF, BFAWU, CWU, FBU, UCATT, TSSA, and the two largest unions, Unison and Unite. By comparison CLP support for his challenger, Owen Smith, was considerably reduced compared to that of Corbyn's leading opponents in 2015. Smith had the support of just 53 of the 338 CLPs which nominated – less than half the number who backed either Burnham or Cooper in 2015. Smith was also supported by the GMB and USDAW, both unions traditionally on the right, and the smaller Community and the Musicians' Union. On 21 August over 640,000 ballot papers went out – to 350,000 paid up members, 168,000 individuals in affiliated organisations, and 129,000 supporters who'd registered at £25 a go. Over half a million people voted in Labour's leadership election. Registered supporters account for more than £3.2 million flowing into the party's coffers – another token of how serious support for Corbyn is.

The leftward shift among party members was confirmed by the results in the election of constituency section representatives to Labour's National Executive Committee. For the first time ever, all six Centre Left Grassroots Alliance candidates were elected. Another interesting feature of these elections was the geographical shift, with all but one of the constituency seats going to out-of-London candidates. The CLGA fielded only one candidate from London, compared to the Progress slate, support for which is believed to be strongest in London.

AUTHENTICITY

The statistics are impressive, but statistics alone cannot explain Corbyn's extraordinary rise. Understanding his attractive power needs qualitative as well as quantitative evaluation. Corbyn's authenticity is at the heart of his popularity. His campaign slogan, 'Jeremy Corbyn: straight talking, honest politics' was well chosen. His flaws as well as his strengths are crucial to understanding his success. No fiery orator, Corbyn's delivery is calm and direct, perhaps a bit dogged at times. Even when the issue's difficult and his views controversial, there have been few opportunities to fault him for failing to say what he means. This is refreshing, a welcome relief from a generation of 'charismatic' politicians who equate debate with controversy and avoid it with soothing ambiguities.

Failing to grasp the importance of Corbyn's warts-and-all appeal, or even respect it, Labour opponents have been openly contemptuous of what they've dubbed his shambolic style. Taking their cue from such comments, the media felt confident about treating him as a loser. The Westminster bubble has paid scant attention to his clear mandate to lead. One dramatic reality check came during the EU referendum. Corbyn was hammered by the Labour remain camp for his so-called failure to make his voice heard – though in reality he was persistently under-reported. Tired of the press pack's dismissive attitude,

Corbyn supporters were captured on camera during a live news conference hissing and booing the BBC's political editor Laura Kuenssberg.

Another blast of reality came with the demands for his resignation that followed the Brexit vote. Under unrelenting pressure, Corbyn calmly refused to back down. Finally, it took the leadership challenge to really drive the point home – exposing the extent to which Corbyn's support had not merely held out but grown, while that of his opponents had weakened. Two *Guardian* letter writers, academic economists, summed up the material basis for 'Corbynism': 'Corbyn does not come across as a wild revolutionary...but rather as a cool observer of what needs to be done to improve life and the economy in Britain today. Unlike recent Labour leaders, Corbyn is untainted by support for the austerity delusion that Labour's fiscal irresponsibility was responsible for the financial crisis of 2008.'

POLICIES

More than his style or presentation, it's Corbyn's policies which appeal to a large cross section of society – not just the Labour left or society's most disenfranchised, but also to a great many 'ordinary working people' (to deploy a much-overused phrase) – people who until recently felt secure, who think of themselves as part of the middle classes perhaps, but are increasingly feeling the pinch of an economic order that cannot deliver the good life.

Corbyn offers hope of a genuine, anti-austerity politics, central to the 'kinder' society he talks about. The mainstream media might underreport him, nonetheless he and his team *are* elaborating a do-able collection of policies which chime with most people's everyday concerns. His proposals for housing, education, health, transport, jobs are circulating by word of mouth and by social media. Corbyn would invest in more council housing, stop privatisation of the health service, take the railways back into public ownership, reinstate the Education

Maintenance Allowance and maintenance grants for students from poorer families ...the list grows. Early in the 2016 leadership campaign, Corbyn identified 10 key commitments that a Labour government led by him would introduce. In summary they were:

- invest £500 billion in infrastructure, manufacturing and new industries, backed up by a publicly-owned National Investment Bank, to generate a million good quality jobs across UK regions and nations;
- build at least half a million council homes in five years, introducing rent controls, secure tenancies and a charter of private tenants' rights, and increase access to affordable home ownership;
- introduce stronger employment rights from day one in a job, end exploitative zero hours contracts and create new employment and trade union rights;
- end health service privatisation, integrate social care for older and disabled people into the NHS, and ensure parity for mental health services;
- establish a new National Education Service to provide access to life-long learning, create universal public childcare, guarantee quality apprenticeships and adult skills training, and progressively restore free education;
- take Britain's fair share of action to meet the Paris climate agreement, accelerate the transition to a low-carbon economy, encourage the expansion of the green industries and jobs via a National Investment Bank, and curb energy bill rises for households;
- rebuild public services and expand democratic participation, including public investment to deliver wealth across regions and nations, insourcing public and local council services, increase access to leisure, arts and sports, expand publicly-controlled bus networks and return the railways into public ownership;
- make sure wealth and the highest earners are fairly taxed, act

against executive pay excess and shrink the gap between the highest and lowest paid;

– respect the human rights of all citizens and protect them from discrimination and prejudice, including tackling violence against women and girls, racism and faith-based discrimination, secure real equality for LGBT and disabled people, and guarantee full rights for EU citizens living and working in Britain.

These are cautious, economically attainable and sustainable policies. Shadow Chancellor John McDonnell, a key Corbyn ally, has made clear from day one of his appointment that Labour's approach to setting economic policies will be sober. McDonnell explained early on: 'Socialism is about planning, and planning is about making sure every penny is spent effectively. Every penny misspent is being taken away from the real investment that is needed.' McDonnell calls George Osborne's Charter for Budget Responsibility a farce. Every year 'the Chancellor misses the targets he set himself' and has to try again. Pointing to his own record as chair of the Greater London Council's Finance Committee in the 1980s, McDonnell makes clear a Corbyn government will balance the books. McDonnell will concentrate on improving productivity, borrowing to fund public investment which will help regenerate the flagging British economy. But his 'fiscal credibility rule' will mean tax revenues are balanced against day-to-day spending over a five-year cycle.

Corbyn's platform is anti-war as well as anti-austerity. The last of his 10 pledges reads: 'We will put conflict resolution and human rights at the heart of foreign policy, commit to working through the United Nations, end support for aggressive wars of intervention and back effective action to alleviate the refugee crisis. British foreign policy has long failed to be either truly independent or internationally cooperative, making the country less safe and reducing our diplomatic and moral authority. We will build human rights and social justice into trade policy, honour our international treaty obligations on nuclear disarmament and encourage others to do the same.'

Foreign policy plays as important a role in Corbyn's political framework as his anti-austerity approach does in the domestic political agenda he wants to set. Unlike many Labour MPs, Corbyn has maintained a substantial interest in, and knowledge of, foreign affairs throughout his political life. His stance has been consistent: advocating an approach which is unaligned, independent of all big power blocs, and anti-imperialist. In a recorded conversation with this author in October 2013, he stressed, for example:

> 'I was strongly opposed to intervention in Iraq. Not because I was a sympathiser of Saddam Hussein and his abuse of human rights. Indeed, I was a lonely voice in the 1980s opposing arms being sent to Iraq and his use of gas at Halabja.'

The latter, a reference to Saddam Hussein's chemical weapons attack on the Kurdish town of Halabja in 1988, is a good illustration of how well briefed he is on foreign affairs. Corbyn described it at the time as 'without precedent since Hiroshima'. On 25 March, within days of the news of Halabja breaking, he was on his feet in the Commons calling on the government to help bring the Iran-Iraq war to an end, and highlighting that 'almost every government in every industrial country is guilty of directly providing arms to one side or the other'. He was able to give details of what had happened, quoting from a letter delivered to the prime minister the previous day: 'about 21,000 ordinary men, women and children from the Halabja population died immediately under the cyanide bombardment. Another 20,000 have been fatally affected and between 300 and 500 are now dying each day.' Corbyn has referred to Halabja again and again in speeches, including those he made against the Gulf War of 1991. And in 2003, on the eve of the invasion of Iraq, Corbyn tabled an Early Day Motion marking the 15th anniversary of the massacre while rejecting the invasion of Iraq.

OPPONENTS

Despite all indications to the contrary, a small but influential Labour clique continue to insist that Corbyn is unelectable: their objective to topple him, their tactic to sling enough mud for some to stick. This gambit delights the media and plays straight into the hands of the government. The fact that Corbyn's support is strong among party members and registered supporters does not, of course, mean the next general election is in the bag. But neither is it the case – as some opponents would have us believe – that party members are wildly out of touch with 'real people'. They *are* real people, some of the many millions who want a political leadership with practical alternatives and a chance to form the next government.

Opinion polls tend to back this up. They're just not getting much coverage in the national media. According to YouGov polling, in February 2016, amidst on-going publicity about Corbyn's difficulties in forming a shadow cabinet, he was trailing 20 points behind Prime Minister David Cameron in the approval ratings. By April however, just six months after he was elected leader, Corbyn was already edging past Cameron. In July, an Ipsos Mori poll showed Labour with 38% support compared to the Tories' 33%. You'd be forgiven, however, for not having noticed that Labour was five points ahead of the Conservatives. The majority of the mainstream media ran with the poll's estimate of voting intentions – calculated using the data from only those respondents who said they were certain to vote – which showed the Tories ahead by one point.

Charley Allan, a Labour activist and *Morning Star* columnist, points out: 'In fact, the figures for "all giving a voting intention," which show Labour's five-point lead, are what most polling companies use as a headline. But I faced an online backlash after tweeting them, with furious JezWeHaters arguing in favour of the narrow Tory lead promoted by Mori.' As Allan also points out, trade unions have protested on a number of occasions that the opinions of trade unionists highlighted by the media have been both unrepresentative of their members and misrepresented by anti-Corbyn sources.

The distortion of Ipsos Mori data is but one among many examples of the media cherry picking opinion polls to fit their 'unelectable Corbyn' storylines. The same may be said for the way in which Corbyn and his opponents are reported or not. One such 'highlight' of the leadership contest between him and Smith, was the latter's botched attempt to out-socialist Corbyn by calling on live TV for ISIS to participate in Syrian peace talks. As the iNews blogger Liam Young observed, Smith's comments demonstrated 'either a serious lapse of moral and historical judgement, or a pathetic attempt to woo those (such as myself) who advocate an anti-interventionist policy'. They should, said Young, disqualify Smith from contesting this leadership race given competency was the cornerstone of his campaign. As one Facebook user quipped: 'If anybody did get around the table with ISIS one wonders how many would come out alive'.

Corbyn on the other hand, asked in the same TV debate if ISIS should be included in talks, replied with a simple 'no'. Smith and his team were forced into some hasty backtracking. In almost any other circumstances you'd reasonably expect such a mega-gaffe by a newsworthy politician to hit the headlines. But quite the contrary: the story went pretty quiet pretty quickly. For the next 24 hours, most reports of that particular debate concentrated on Corbyn's inability to recall who Ant and Dec were. No satisfactory explanation has been offered as to why Corbyn's failure to recognise the names of a comedy duo merits greater coverage than Smith's ISIS remarks.

The *Daily Mail*'s resident right-wing heavy, columnist Richard Littlejohn, was one of those who took Corbyn to task for his bafflement. But to give discredit where discredit's due, Littlejohn's barrel-scraping does merit a mention. Not a peep in his 500-word rant about the gaffe by 'Owen Wossname' (of more interest, apparently, was his inability to remember the Wales football team's score over Belgium in the recent Euro-

pean championships), but Littlejohn did manage a sideswipe at
Corbyn who should apologise for recognising Hamas and Hez-
bollah. With daily dirt-raking against Corbyn, and by extension
the party, Labour was still five points up on a Tory government,
one that's learned some PR lessons from the Corbyn election
and ditched its nasty-rich-boy leadership for one that appears –
on the surface, at least – sensible, hardworking, state-educated
and altogether more in touch.

With four years to go before the next general election has
to be called, the possibilities of events outside the control of
any politicians sparking a public mood swing are all but end-
less. But there is also time for the Labour team to flesh out the
details of its policies for government and make a strong, popular and economically sound case to the electorate. The space
to do so requires different conditions *within* the Labour Party
– and Corbyn's opponents know it. Behind the media attacks on
Corbyn are the remnants of the New Labour project grouped
around Progress – and more recently Saving Labour and Labour Tomorrow. This wing of the party prefers to see Labour
kept out of government rather than see a resurgence of left-
wing ideas and influence.

Though small in number, they are well-connected and able
to wield considerable influence around Westminster, not only
among the PLP but also in anti-Labour circles that benefit from
their activities. Their public face includes figures such as:
- **Tony Blair**, who told a Progress meeting during the 2015
  leadership election that Corbyn should never be allowed to
  become prime minister. Blair said of Corbyn's platform: 'It's
  not that it wouldn't win power. I personally think it's unlikely.
  But even if you did, it wouldn't be right. It wouldn't take the
  country forwards; it would take it backwards. That's why it's
  not the right thing to do. When people say my heart says I
  should really be with that politics – well get a transplant.'
- **Alastair Campbell**, who's repeated Blair's don't vote Labour
  message. He told the BBC: 'I would find it very difficult to put

a cross on the ballot paper if the consequence of that was to make Jeremy Corbyn prime minister of this country.'

– **David Blunkett**, Blair's former Home Secretary who says Labour will be 'annihilated' if Corbyn leads the party in a general election, who's called on Corbyn and the Momentum 'fringe group' to set up their own party and is now heading up Saving Labour.

– **John McTernan**, another Blair advisor who said that 'the Labour Party was stabbed in the heart and killed' by the NEC's decision to have Corbyn on the 2016 leadership ballot. A Progress regular, he's been on the stump around Britain for months, warning of a Soviet (ooops! nowadays it's Russian) renaissance unless Labour backed the Trident replacement.

– **Luke Akehurst**, a New Labour come-lately, is another Progress stalwart who describes himself variously as 'a grassroots campaigner for Israel', 'not Jewish but I'm a Zionist', and committed 'to fight against Hard Left factionalism'. He is also secretary of Labour First, a grouping of the trade union right that campaigns for NATO and the US special relationship. In the 2015 general election, Akehurst argued 'the UK's strategic nuclear deterrent needs to be a red line for Labour' in the event of a hung parliament.

You don't have to be a conspiracy theorist to start feeling that groups in the Labour Party are hatching plots against Corbyn. The *en bloc* resignations from Corbyn's cabinet which precipitated the leadership contest, brought home to many how planned and organised the opposition to Corbyn really is. As the 2016 leadership campaign advanced, however, Progress became strangely quiet. As broadcaster and Corbyn supporter Paul Mason quipped: 'The Progress website looks like it's being maintained by interns, while there are no official Progress events being held until the day after the leadership election (Angela Eagle and a venture capitalist).'

It's difficult, no doubt, for New Labour to explain its backing for a candidate whose main strategy has been to out-socialist Corbyn. New Labour's get-Corbyn-out baton was picked up by Saving Labour, an organisation which has blossomed fleetingly for a mere couple of weeks in July. It too made no mention of Owen Smith, and has been replaced by something that promises to be altogether darker, Labour Tomorrow, which is offering to distribute funds to 'moderate centre-left organisations which are committed to rebuilding a consensus for a Labour government'. Or as Tom Blenkinsop's tweets obligingly clarify: 'Corbynites, Momentum and the rest of the hard left get out of the people's party'.

Despite a decisive vote for Corbyn in the 2016 leadership challenge, rumours abound about what the anti-Corbyn PLP might try next. Will shadow cabinet resignees unresign? Some have already indicated their willingness to stand again. It's a difficult strategy, especially for senior figures whose resignation statements were so publicly expressed, but contradictory behaviour hasn't deterred them to date. Are reselections of Corbyn-hating MPs really that likely, as some MPs keep insisting? Some of his opponents have been said to be considering legal action to claim the Labour name, or will some Labour MPs form a breakaway group in parliament? And how will the much-discussed call for shadow cabinet elections end?

A full split is also being talked about in the media and on the fringes of the party. There have been two past experiences – when Ramsay MacDonald and part of the parliamentary party joined a national government with Conservatives and Liberals in 1931, and the Gang of Four's departure in 1981 to form the Social Democratic Party. Both were bad. Labour opposition to Corbyn, its likely impact and future, is considered further in the final chapter.

BANNING THE BOMB

As the brief outline of the anti-Corbyn wing of the party above suggests, his opposition to nuclear weapons is one of the primary factors driving his opponents. Nuclear disarmament, the theme of this book, occupies a central role within Corbyn's foreign policy framework. He is a life-long member of the Campaign for Nuclear Disarmament. When he became Labour leader, he was a vice chair of CND, actively engaged in the day to day running of the campaign. In an interview soon thereafter, Corbyn told BBC Radio 4 *Today* programme's seven million plus listeners that if he became prime minister he would not press the nuclear button. 'There are five declared nuclear weapon states in the world. There are three others that have nuclear weapons,' Corbyn explained. 'That is eight countries out of 192; 187 countries do not feel the need to have nuclear weapons to protect their security. Why should those five need them? We are not in the cold war any more. I don't think we should be spending £100 billion on renewing Trident.'

The cries of outrage are still echoing round the corridors of power.

In a recorded conversation with me in October 2013, Corbyn described the place of nuclear disarmament in his political framework as:

'a passion since school, being opposed to the horrors of nuclear weapons and war. The film *The War Game* had a big effect on me, and also I remember the Cuban missile crisis very well... I remember being involved in a lot of international issues at the time, not just nuclear disarmament.'

He explained that his opposition to the bomb and his interest in politics had developed early and simultaneously:

'I grew up in rural Shropshire, in a swing constituency, the Wrekin. Mum and dad were both members of the Labour Party and had met campaigning for the Spanish Republic in the 1930s. So there was a Labour left tradition in the household, though they weren't particularly politically active when I was a child. I became active first in environmental and animal rights issues. It was a hunting and shooting area and I was the only one in my class against fox hunting.

'I joined the Campaign for Nuclear Disarmament when I was 15 and the first demonstrations I went on were anti-nuclear ones. I went on one of the last Aldermaston demonstrations of the 1960s. It was very memorable to me, a young lad up from the sticks. I joined the Labour Party around that time, 1965-66, despite my anger at Harold Wilson over Vietnam. Although I don't think many of us realised his political support was a trade-off for not sending troops.

'I campaigned in the '64 and '66 elections. I was very active as secretary and then chair of Wrekin Young Socialists, and Labour candidate in the school election. I left school in 1967 and went abroad for two years for VSO [Voluntary Service Overseas] in Jamaica, then travelling around Latin America.'

Corbyn's views on nuclear weapons are typical of many on the left of the party. Walter Wolfgang, a former member of Labour's National Executive Committee, summarises the Labour left's position thus:

'Labour made a major mistake by lining up behind one of the two power blocs which emerged at the end of WWII. The US-Soviet conflict was a classical power conflict. Britain shouldn't have got involved. But it lined up with the United States from the start.'

Throughout its history, the Labour Party has claimed a preference for the peaceful resolution of conflicts – in words at least, if not always in deeds. Clement Attlee, for example, was a United Nations supporter with a preference for cooperation rather than conflict – a perspective underlined in Labour's 1945 manifesto. This didn't stop the Attlee government playing a central role in the acquisition of a British bomb. Three periods in the development of Labour's nuclear weapons policies are considered in the chapters which follow: the role of the Attlee government in developing the British bomb; the evolution of policy in the 1980s-90s; and the contemporary debate over Trident replacement. Some of the same characteristics are clear and present in all three periods, offering insight perhaps about where today's struggle over Labour nuclear weapons policy might or might not lead.

CHAPTER 2
Labour and the origins of the British bomb

Labour's present-day controversy over Trident is not new. The adherence to nuclear weapons by successive Labour leaderships has been a constant bugbear, starting with Clement Attlee's decision to build a 'British' bomb. The physicist Lord Rutherford was the first to split the atom in a controlled experiment in 1917, generating theoretical investigation in scientific circles of its potential as a 'super weapon'. Practical work on an atomic bomb began in 1940 when, on the advice of physicists Rudolf Peierls and Otto Frisch, the Conservative government of Neville Chamberlain set up the MAUD (Military Application of Uranium Detonation) Committee.

Chamberlain stood down as prime minister soon after, clearing the way for Winston Churchill's wartime coalition government. Churchill was instrumental in alerting the United States to the feasibility of nuclear weapons and when America set up its own programme in 1942 he sent a team of top scientists over to the Los Alamos Laboratories. He had brought Labour into the heart of government, and by 1942 Attlee had become his deputy. Though Churchill kept the details of Britain's atomic weapons programme secret from his full Cabinet, it is inconceivable that Attlee was unaware of what was going on.

ORIGINS

Attlee continued Britain's nuclear weapons programme after Labour won the 1945 election. He set up his own Cabinet sub-committee, GEN 75 – with Ernest Bevin, also a member of Churchill's War Cabinet and by then Labour's Foreign Secretary; AV Alexander, Minister of Defence; Herbert Morrison, the Deputy Prime Minister and another war-time Cabinet member; and Hugh Dalton, Chancellor of the Exchequer. By the time Churchill returned to office in October 1951, work was well advanced. Attlee like Churchill kept atomic bomb research secret not only from the public, but from most of his Cabinet too. And it was not until October 1952 when Britain's first ever atomic weapons test took place over the Monte Bello Islands off the west coast of Australia, that the Attlee government's decision to build a bomb became known.

Public alarm over Britain's first test combined with growing awareness of what was happening in Hiroshima and Nagasaki to produce the first flickerings of a protest movement. The United States had attempted to censor information about the aftermath of atomic bombing on Hiroshima and Nagasaki, and the American-led administration of post-war Japan had kept a tight rein on what could be reported. But details had begun to circulate by 1952. The first journalist to visit Hiroshima was Wilfred Burchett whose report, 'The Atomic Plague', was printed by the *Daily Express* a month after the bombing; and in 1946 *The New Yorker* had devoted an entire edition to John Hersey's ground-breaking account of the lives of six survivors, continuously in print ever since as the book *Hiroshima*.

By the mid-1950s, concerns about nuclear weapons, especially the health effects of nuclear testing, were being aired even in establishment circles. In March 1955, for example, Dr Edith Summerskill, Labour MP for Fulham and a founder of the Socialist Health Association, led a parliamentary debate on the genetic effects of nuclear explosions. Her resolution expressed fears about 'the dangers facing humanity as a result of continuing radioactive contamination of the world's atmosphere, particularly to future generations'. As knowledge of the devastating effects of atomic weapons spread, concern became protest. In Britain this led to the annual 'Ban the Bomb' marches between London and the Atomic Weapons Establishment at Aldermaston, and the formation of the Campaign for Nuclear Disarmament in 1958. Opposition to nuclear weapons was growing in the Labour Party too. Walter Wolfgang, a former member of Labour's National Executive Committee, then a recent member of the Labour Party, recalls:

> 'Around the time of Britain's first atomic tests many women in particular became concerned about the health dangers of radiation, its effect on unborn children and so on. This was much discussed in scientific journals at the time, and found a reflection in political magazines such as *Tribune* and *New Statesman*. Through opposition to testing, people became aware of the problem with nuclear weapons. Then politicos such as myself got involved, concerned about Britain's foreign policies and international relationships. There was coalescence between the two that led to the foundation of the Campaign for Nuclear Disarmament. There were lots of people in the campaign who were Labour sympathisers.'

RESERVATIONS

The extent of Labour's 1945 election victory meant Attlee commanded a handsome parliamentary majority of 148. On a high turnout, almost half of all votes had been cast for Labour; and a 12% swing saw the party's 166 seats rise to 393. Labour's programme of radical domestic reform had won the landslide, and ensured strong support for the government from Labour MPs, party members and trade unionists alike. Labour was now in a position to implement some of the labour movement's chief demands – full employment and a programme of public ownership. In these circumstances, Attlee faced few serious challenges from within the labour movement in the course of the 1940s.

Initial reservations over government policy took the form of misgivings about foreign policy. Some Labour MPs and constituency parties voiced concerns about tying Britain so closely to one of the two major protagonists in the unfolding Cold War and about Bevin's commitment to what was to become the North Atlantic Treaty. Alignment with the United States was deemed to be an unnecessary spur to confrontation. Opposition to Atlanticism was neither a pacifist nor a crypto-communist perspective, as its opponents claimed, but a manifestation of the belief that negotiated solutions are preferable and more enduring than enforced settlements. Furthermore, non-alignment tapped into a sense of war fatigue among the UK population and the widely-held desire for peace. The USSR's decisive contribution to Allied victory in WWII was widely respected. Soviet troops had fought the German invasion in appalling conditions, and over 26 million Soviet citizens had lost their lives. The language of the American and European media at the time indicates this, with references to 'our heroic Soviet allies' and 'Uncle Joe' Stalin in magazines such as *Punch* and *Life*.

Reservations over the Attlee government's convergence with the US were intensified by fears about the impact that continued high arms spending would have on Labour's domestic agenda. And a series of crises in the British economy were inhibiting the government's domestic reform programme, adding weight to these concerns. But after 1947, international events – such as the communist rise to power in Czechoslovakia and the Berlin blockade – combined with anti-communist propaganda to mute antipathy to the government's Cold War-oriented stance. Doubts about Britain's role in the growing confrontation between the USA and USSR were reignited, however, by the announcement of a huge British rearmament programme in 1950, as Attlee came under American pressure to increase Britain's contribution to the Korean War.

LEFT CHALLENGES

The main challenges to Attlee from within the party were mounted over foreign policy. A hint of the opposition from local parties can be judged, for example, by the terms of a motion to Labour's 1946 annual conference that attacked the government's 'continuation of traditional Conservative foreign policies'. It was withdrawn after Bevin claimed it was a motion of censure against him. Opposition also surfaced in parliament. Favouring a collegiate style of government, Attlee had set up policy committees of backbench Labour MPs to liaise with ministers. The foreign policy committee gave him most trouble. In November 1946, Richard Crossman attempted to amend the King's speech, urging the government to 'review and recast its conduct of international affairs as to... provide a democratic and constructive socialist alternative to an otherwise inevitable conflict between American capitalism and Soviet communism'.

Rising dissatisfaction prompted the formation of the Keep Left group, the most influential but not the only left caucus around at that time. Named after its 1947 manifesto which was co-authored by Crossman with fellow MPs Ian Mikardo, Michael Foot, Konni Zilliacus and others, Keep Left made the case for a European 'third force' and floated the idea of nuclear disarmament. 'The task of British socialism must be, wherever possible, to save the smaller nations from this futile ideological warfare and to heal the breach between the USA and the USSR. But we cannot do this if we ourselves have taken sides either in a Communist bloc or in an anti-Bolshevik axis.' In May 1949 three Labour MPs, Konni Zilliacus, John Platts-Mills and Tom Braddock, did vote against Britain ratifying the new treaty: 'this House approves the North Atlantic Treaty signed in Washington on 4 April, 1949, relating to the promotion of stability and wellbeing in the North Atlantic area and to collective defence for the preservation of peace and security'.

Keep Left maintained its distinctive stance on foreign policy and continued to oppose Bevin's anti-communism. *Tribune*, the newspaper of the Labour left founded in 1937, also opposed Labour's foreign policy, and there was considerable overlap between the leading members of both. But a split was looming in the heterogeneous ranks of the Labour left. Mikardo, who exercised considerable influence within the party, continued to argue for a third way; but Michael Foot did not. Under Foot's editorship, 1948-52, *Tribune* retreated from a third way position and took an anti-Soviet stance, such as supporting a ban on communists holding office in the transport workers union. Reinforced in his views by the failure of the Hungarian uprising, Foot became a supporter of NATO. Nevertheless he and *Tribune* continued to campaign for nuclear disarmament and helped found CND.

THE BEVANITES

Though NATO membership divided the Labour left, they were united on rearmament – the terrain of the next confrontation with the Attlee government during its brief second term. Labour had won the February 1950 general election with a slim five-seat majority. The outbreak of the Korean War in June brought increased pressure from the US for British rearmament, and early in 1951 the new Chancellor, Hugh Gaitskell announced a £4.7 billion increase in military expenditure (around £150 billion in today's prices). It was a doubling of the military budget that amounted to 14% of gross domestic product. To help pay for this, Gaitskell proposed to freeze the health budget – by cutting hospital spending and introducing charges for prescriptions, dentures and spectacles.

Aneurin Bevan, Minister of Labour, led the opposition telling Cabinet colleagues that 'it would be undesirable in principle, and politically dangerous, for the Labour Party thus to abandon the conception of a free Health Service'. He resigned when the Cabinet backed Gaitskell, along with two other ministers: Harold Wilson, then President of the Board of Trade, and John Freeman from the Ministry of Supply. Still a much-discussed episode of Labour history, it's clear with hindsight that Bevan and Wilson were right on the main issue, and Gaitskell wrong. With barely any wiggle room, Attlee was facing difficult economic and social choices, and growing disquiet on the Labour backbenches and in the constituencies. In the October 1951 election Labour paid dear for its attachment to the politics of grandeur, with a net loss of 20 seats. The party was out of government for the next 13 years, until Wilson's victory in 1964. You will still hear it claimed that Nye Bevan's resignation, rather than the government's rearmament policy, lost Labour that election.

Meanwhile, his resignation as Minister of Health galvanised the left in the local parties. Bevan was supported by many leading figures in the Parliamentary Labour Party – including Crossman, Foot, Mikardo, and Barbara Castle as well as Wilson and Freeman – the first meeting of the Bevanite group took place just a couple of weeks after the ministerial resignations. Keep Left joined forces with them and *Tribune* contributed a flow of material critical of rearmament. The Bevanites' most notable parliamentary rebellion was in March 1952, when 57 Labour MPs broke the whip to vote against the Conservative government's defence estimates. They were in tune with the mood of the party, and on the whole the constituencies lined up behind Bevan. At Labour's annual conference that year, CLP delegates expressed their disapproval of rearmament by inflicting defeat on the leadership in the NEC elections. Morrison and Dalton, both long-serving constituency reps, were replaced by Crossman and Wilson. Six of the seven CLP places were held by Bevanites. The Labour establishment was seriously shaken. Accustomed to years of docile conferences, the Labour right were incensed, and there are many reports of the noisy and bad-tempered atmosphere that prevailed.

During Attlee's governments, the right had exercised effective control over all Labour's ruling bodies – the Cabinet, the National Executive, and annual conference – facilitated by the loyalty of constituency parties. Relations between the parliamentary leadership and those of the major trade unions were close knit, and the unions' interventionist approach to the party consolidated the Labour right's control. Three union figures formed the core of this support: transport workers leader Arthur Deakin, Tom Williamson of the general and municipal workers, and Will Lawther of the mineworkers. As the latter put it 'between us there is understanding and common sense'. This 'understanding' included a shared definition of the 'enemy' – communism in all its forms. Lewis Minkin, the unsurpassed historian of British trade unionism, confirms that right-wing union leaders believed the Communist Party was behind the Bevanite movement.

John Edmonds, GMB General Secretary from 1986 to 2003, explains his union's position in the post-war period:

> 'My predecessor but one, Jack Cooper [1963-73] was very much part of the Deakin-Williamson-Bevin tradition – solid on defence, got to maintain the independent nuclear deterrent, and so on. So the union was very much on that side of the debate. It was a closed debate, and Jack Cooper was keen not to open it up. His successor, David Basnett [1973-1986], who was inclined away from that tradition, had great difficulty. He wanted to try and shift the union, but the Cooper position was still very strongly in place. And that was also how it was in the T&G, sustained by the GMW [later renamed GMB] ... until Kinnock's leadership of the party [when] nuclear disarmament was a live debate.'

Rodney Bickerstaffe, General Secretary of NUPE from 1982, and then its successor UNISON, until 2000, tells another story:

> 'Right from the word go there was a big majority in favour of peace and nuclear disarmament in NUPE. The first motions started going to Labour conference in the 1950s.

When a nuclear disarmament motion was carried for just one year in 1960, we were one of the eight unions that supported it. We had a left leadership at the time, in fact we always had a left leadership.'

The net result of the tight relationship at the top of the party and the unions was that the Attlee government faced little if any effective challenge. Bevanism was a break with this, and its emergence was greeted with vigorous accusations of irresponsibility and disloyalty. Walter Wolfgang recalls one instance of this, which gives a flavour of how the party leadership responded to challenges. In 1950 he was elected secretary of his Labour Party branch, part of the outer London Richmond CLP. With local approval, he set about organising his very first Labour Party public meeting:

'It was a conference on the Korean War, to air everyone's views. But the right got wind of it. The regional organiser came to Richmond and banned the conference, calling me a Trotskyite. I was absolutely crestfallen, and it's the only time in my whole life I got deliberately drunk! It was an important and formative political experience for me.'

TRADE UNIONS

Foreign policy was an important area of difference, but not the only issue of concern to the unions. Labour plans for the NHS, housing, and industrial relations were also under pressure. The problems of the union-party relationship were exemplified in the different stances of Ernest Bevin and Aneurin Bevan. Overall, the first decade of post-war Britain was one of stability in Labour Party-trade union relations. But the redistribution of wealth and power was not as fundamental as the government's legislative programme had promised. Industrial relations became increasingly tense, driven in part by the Labour government's response to a series of economic crises, and magnified by a pay freeze and the rearmament programme. Beginning in 1956 when Frank Cousins, a committed nuclear disarmer, became the left-wing leader of the Transport and General Workers Union the trade union left grew in influence both in the trade union movement and the Labour Party. By then, Bevan himself had shifted his position on arms spending and nuclear weapons.

Like Britain's rearmament during the Korean War, the Labour leadership's support for German rearmament brought howls of protest from the constituencies. In April 1954 Bevan resigned again, this time from the Shadow Cabinet, when it decided to support the government. Annual conference that year saw 58 resolutions opposing German rearmament. The one that was debated condemned 'all proposals for German rearmament'. It was narrowly defeated when the woodworkers union changed their vote; and the NEC's position that Germany should 'contribute to collective security' was passed by an equally small margin. But the left's success in the 1952 conference proved to be the highpoint of the Bevanites' power inside the party. In the 1954 election for National Treasurer, in which all sections of the party voted – MPs, trade unions and constituencies – Gaitskell defeated Bevan by a big majority. When Attlee retired as leader after the 1955 general election defeat, Gaitskell won the leadership in the first round.

PARALLELS

There are some striking similarities, then and now. But there are important differences too – between the circumstances in the country, the relation of forces in the party, but most especially between Corbyn and the faltering champion of nuclear disarmament, Nye Bevan. In his short time as leader Corbyn has already been compared to Kier Hardy, George Lansbury, Clem Attlee, Nye Bevan, and of course Michael Foot – depending on the instigators' own standpoints and the particular lesson they urged us to draw.

Parallels with Attlee's style don't go amiss, though policy

similarities are less clear. Attlee was quiet, economical rather than rhetorical in the speeches he made, and famously modest. An amusing example of the latter characteristic was given in a review of a recently-published Attlee biography which appeared in the *London Review of Books*. Sixteen years into retirement, Attlee was canvassed during the 1967 general election by students who failed to recognise him. Would he be voting Labour they asked? His terse reply: 'already a member'. In a world where every utterance, however dreary, helps fill a 24/7 news culture, Corbyn sometimes catches interviewers unawares with direct, single phrase answers.

Whilst the Attlee government's Britain shares certain characteristics with society today, the dissimilarities are much more striking. In 1945 the world was emerging from war, exhausted but relieved at the prospect of peace, and Britain was in the hands of a new government that promised dramatic improvements in people's everyday lives. The overarching mood was one of optimism. The world of 2015-16, by contrast, is chaotic – no end in sight to the wars in the Middle East and North Africa which are the breeding ground for terrorist violence on the streets of Europe and beyond, and near astronomical numbers of people fleeing war and poverty with no solutions on the table. In Britain the prospect of economic insecurity and declining living standards for the majority stands in contrast to the cocooned lives of a privileged few, and no party of government seems capable of coming to grips with this inequality. The dominant British mood is that of pessimism.

BAN THE BOMB

Despite the decline of the Bevanites from the mid-1950s, opposition to nuclear weapons continued to grow – among the public and in the Labour Party. Nye Bevan himself held fast to the third-way perspective of Keep Left, supporting the non-alignment movement. No supporter of the Soviet Union, he thought foreign policy and domestic necessity were intertwined. Threats to freedom were no longer direct and aggressive, as they'd been in the 1930s: 'world peace and social progress at home are two sides of the same coin'. Bevan argued the chief weapons of the Soviet Union were economic, social and ideological rather than military. It was this belief which led him to champion the cause of nuclear disarmament: 'The atom bomb is no answer. That is a constant factor.' But when Gaitskell took over as leader, Bevan began to rebuild his bridges with the leadership. He rejoined the Shadow Cabinet first as Colonial Secretary, then as Shadow Foreign Secretary and was elected national treasurer of the party. Three years later, in 1957, he became deputy leader until ill-health forced him to stand down.

The struggle over nuclear weapons policy between the constituencies and the leadership continued to gain steam, and the number of resolutions to Labour's annual conference grew year on year. In 1956, conference passed a resolution expressing concern about the dangers of radioactive contamination, opposing nuclear explosions and declaring that 'the Labour Party should work towards the abolition of all nuclear weapons'. In 1957, 127 nuclear weapons resolutions were submitted and conference debated one which called on Labour not to test or produce nuclear weapons. As Foreign Secretary, Nye Bevan replied to the debate on behalf of the leadership. He shocked his supporters with a now-notorious speech in which he opposed the resolution, urging delegates not to send the Foreign Secretary 'naked into the conference chamber'. That speech turned conference round; the resolution was overwhelmingly defeated. The reasons for his about-face continue to be debated – from the assertion in Foot's biography that Bevan was neither a unilateralist nor a supporter of the Soviet Union, to the view that his change of heart represented a softened emphasis on class antagonism that removed his opposition to US and British imperialism.

Bevan's renunciation of nuclear disarmament did not deter its Labour supporters, and opposition to nuclear weapons remained closely associated with foreign policy concerns. The

Bevanites were not the only anti-nuclear weapons grouping in the party. Others included Labour Peace Fellowship (nowadays Labour Action for Peace) and Victory for Socialism (VfS) which set up the H-bomb Campaign Committee jointly with the Movement for Colonial Freedom (now Liberation). These two got the first Aldermaston march off the ground alongside the Direct Action Committee. Founded in 1944 by father and son team Frederick and Eric Messer, one of VfS's better-known supporters was Fenner Brockway, a founder member of CND. Walter Wolfgang recalls:

'I met Eric Messer at a Peace with China meeting in Bloomsbury. He was active in Victory for Socialism and invited me to one of its meetings. VfS was a response to the Labour government's foreign policy and its compromises on social policy. Their objectives seemed to match mine – the pursuit of peace abroad and an extension of public ownership and worker participation at home. So I became an active member. I joined the committee and was even its secretary for a time.

'Victory for Socialism was quite small, but it had a number of MPs associated with it – such as Geoffrey Bing, Bill Warby, and Stephen Swingler. It recruited rank and file members mainly from the CLPs, but some trade unionists who were members of affiliated unions also joined. There were a few senior figures from unions associated with it. VfS had a membership, a regular newsletter; it held conferences, and threw off wider campaigns. These were not sub-committees but separate campaigns, designed to involve Labour Party members on a particular issue who didn't necessarily want to be associated with all the policies of VfS.

'I met Hugh Jenkins, who later became chair of CND, as a result of my involvement in VfS. In 1954 Hugh, Olive Bentley and I co-authored a VfS pamphlet, *In Pursuit of*

Peace, which attempted to set out some principles for Britain's role in the world – a reduction in the arms burden, an increase in trade with the east, and an end to dependence on exporting arms to NATO countries. Compared to the stances we took later, the policies the pamphlet advocated were very mild indeed. Basically we argued the line of Nye Bevan that Britain shouldn't be too closely aligned with the United States.'

Wolfgang became joint secretary of the VfS's Suez Emergency Committee and helped set up a Trafalgar Square rally in 1956. The Labour Party as a whole opposed the invasion and the leadership agreed to take over organising the event, which saw 20-30,000 gather in protest at the Anthony Eden government's military action against Egypt. VfS was campaigning on more controversial terrain when it set up the H-Bomb Campaign Committee, however:

'After Suez, there was increasing concern about the testing and proliferation of nuclear weapons, and Hugh Jenkins and I helped set up the VfS's Hydrogen Bomb Campaign Committee. We held another demonstration in Trafalgar Square just before the start of Labour's 1957 annual conference and marched to Hyde Park – something unusual in those days. The rally was addressed by Barbara Castle among others. Like most of the members of the H-Bomb Committee she wasn't a unilateralist, and neither was I. My concern was about a war between NATO and the Warsaw Pact. Nuclear weapons could make that war more likely and more dangerous.

'I thought the US-Soviet conflict was a classical power conflict and Britain shouldn't get involved. We should adopt the principles of the United Nations charter, and not associate ourselves with either side. But Britain was lined up with the US from the start. NATO was a consequence of

US-Soviet rivalry, so I opposed its formation. It meant that divisions between the two parts of Europe would be even more tightly drawn.

'Campaigning on the H-bomb grew out of these concerns. My critique of the UK's role in the Cold War preceded my commitment to unilateral nuclear disarmament. Hugh Jenkins converted me to unilateralism later on. The H-Bomb Committee became unilateralist, and through it I became associated with the New Left – but that's another story.'

SHORT-LIVED VICTORY

Wolfgang's opposition to the role Britain was playing in the Cold War soon placed him squarely in the unilateralist camp. A *Tribune* article evokes the mood at the time of the demonstration. Having nuclear weapons made the UK more vulnerable and was a costly waste of money, it argued, concluding with a call to support the H-bomb Campaign Committee's demonstration. 'Above all, it is wrong. Its use, which would bring us not victory but annihilation, would be a moral crime without equal in history. A campaign to bring these truths home to all Britain can evoke a mighty response. For Labour, there is both an opportunity and a duty. To demand an end to nuclear tests is a first step, but no substitute for tackling the fundamental question of a strategy and a foreign policy based on having the bomb. To call for international agreement to end the atomic arms race is no longer enough; it gives the Tories a chance to escape by lengthy conferences ending in sighs over Russian obstinacy. Labour should say, boldly, that it is time for Britain to lead the world in rejecting the manufacture and use of the H-bomb.'

Three years later, the 1960 Labour conference passed a motion in favour of unilateral nuclear disarmament for the first time. Its adoption reflected both growing disapproval of nuclear weapons and the rise of the trade union left, led by Cousins and the TGWU. Winning policy on nuclear disarmament was an unexpected victory, and the result of some accidental factors. Nevertheless, it is often seen as the first real power struggle between the parliamentary leadership and conference. Gaitskell's hard-nosed response was immediate, pledging to 'fight, fight, and fight again to save the party we love'.

After Labour's defeat in the 1959 election, Gaitskell had set out to 'modernise' the rule book, in line with what he believed to be a social shift from blue- to white-collar employment and the rise of a new middle class – a view elaborated later by sociologists Goldthorpe and Lockwood in their *Affluent Worker* study of car assembly line workers, as the 'embourgeoisement' of the working class. Gaitskell sought to remove Clause IV from Labour's constitution and reduce trade union power in the party. This came to a head in the 1960 conference. Gaitskell had to retreat when he found himself faced by opposition from all sides in the unions – a point driven home when the transport workers threw their support behind unilateral nuclear disarmament, defeating the party's leadership.

NEW MOVEMENT

Labour's internal divisions notwithstanding, the dispute in the party was part of a new international movement, energetic, vociferous and committed to getting rid of all nuclear weapons. Some of the biggest protests of 1950s Europe took place after the Greek government joined NATO and accepted US nuclear weapons on its territory in 1958. The West German movement, which included the Social Democratic Party and the trade unions, called for a nuclear-weapons free zone in Central Europe. There were campaigns against nuclear weapons in Sweden and Switzerland by the mid-1950s, and active nuclear disarmament campaigns in Denmark and Norway by the end of the decade. The exception was France, which became the fourth nuclear weapons state in 1960; its nuclear weapons tests in the atmosphere in 1968 led to global protests and hastened the launch of the French nuclear disarmament movement in the 1970s.

There were even protests in North America. Scientists and politicians in the USA were expressing concern about nuclear testing by the mid-1950s, and tiny but important anti-militarist and pacifist organisations like the American Friends Service Committee and WILPF, the Women's International League for Peace and Freedom, were taking the issue up. As in Britain, the Canadian nuclear disarmament movement had begun with the Committee for the Control of Radiation Hazards in 1958, which called for an end to nuclear testing. Nuclear disarmament movements also grew up in Australia and New Zealand in the 1950s.

But unsurprisingly, the biggest and strongest movement in the Pacific arose in Japan and has maintained momentum over a much longer period. As noted earlier, the Allied Occupation of Japan, 1945-52, imposed strict controls on reporting the effects of the atomic bombing of Hiroshima and Nagasaki. But the authorities couldn't keep the lid on the horrors. Local government and university-backed research resulted in detailed compilations of the damage; and thousands of personal testimonies by hibakusha, the atomic bomb survivors, were written. Japanese anger burst forth when the US conducted its first hydrogen bomb test at Bikini Atoll in March 1954 and radioactive fallout hit the crew of a Japanese fishing vessel. A group of Tokyo women launched an anti-nuclear campaign which had attracted 18 million signatures by November, including about half of the entire population of the district affected.

The first World Conference Against Atomic and Hydrogen Bombs took place the following year, attended by 30,000 Japanese and 54 foreign guests from 12 other countries. Gensuikyo, the association behind the conference, held its 71st such event in 2016. Around 7,400 people from Japan attended alongside delegates from 27 countries, including the UN High Representative for Disarmament Affairs, a former UN High Representative for Disarmament Affairs, and the Vice-Foreign Minister of Mexico.

With the exception of Japan, however, the swell of anger that launched an international nuclear disarmament movement in the 1950s had begun to decline by the mid-1960s, thanks to the signing of the Partial Test Ban Treaty and improvements in US-Soviet relations. It was not to resurface again as a mass movement until the late 1970s.

DÉTENTE

Starting with US-Soviet talks in the aftermath of the 1962 Cuban missile crisis, many came to believe the West was entering a period of steady progress towards nuclear arms control. Optimism was reinforced during Richard Nixon's presidency which saw a further unfreezing of East-West relations. The US was believed to be moving away from the confrontation of early Cold War years, marked by mutually assured destruction, the MAD doctrine – the notion that developing the ability to give as good as they got, to massively retaliate, acted to deter either side from launching a nuclear attack. President John F Kennedy and Soviet General Secretary Nikita Khrushchev engaged in negotiations which resulted in the USSR dismantling its weapons based in Cuba in return for which the US made a public declaration that it would not invade Cuba and secretly agreed to dismantle its uranium tipped, medium-range ballistic missile (MRBM) deployed against the Soviet Union in Turkey and Italy. East-West interaction took a further step forward when Richard Nixon entered the White House in 1969. Nixon also opened relations with the People's Republic of China, withdrew from Vietnam, and engaged in more initiatives to reduce nuclear tensions.

In 1972 a US-Soviet summit in Moscow produced two arms control agreements, proclaimed by Nixon and Soviet First Secretary Leonid Brezhnev as the opening of an era of 'peaceful co-existence'. The Strategic Arms Limitation Treaty (SALT I) froze the number of strategic ballistic missile launchers at existing levels and set limits on the number of submarine and land-based intercontinental missiles in range of the other's borders. The Anti-Ballistic Missiles (ABM) Treaty limited the number of strategic anti-ballistic missile systems each could deploy against intercontinental nuclear attack. Two were allowed: one to defend the capital city; and one to defend the intercontinental ballistic missile (ICBM) silos. By preventing either side from gaining significant advantage over the other, which could have led them to consider the feasibility of a nuclear attack, the ABM Treaty is widely regarded as having kept the nuclear peace for the next 30 years. The Russian Federation took over the obligations of the ABM Treaty when the Soviet Union dissolved at the end of 1991. But President George W Bush unilaterally terminated it in 2002 to pursue developing a new generation of space-based US missile defences. Arms control experts believe Bush's actions delivered a serious blow to the prospects for nuclear disarmament.

Despite progress represented by these treaties, the US and USSR continued to develop their short- and medium-range nuclear programmes –Trident, Pershing and cruise missiles in the US, and SS 20 series in the Soviet Union. Growing unease over these developments, combined with a stepping-up of the US military budget in the latter half of the decade brought the beginnings of a resurgence of the European nuclear disarmament movement. In Britain, the decision to station US cruise missiles on British territory, combined with the election of Ronald Reagan, a bellicose Republican, sparked what's known as the second wave of CND in the early 1980s.

CHAPTER 3
Nuclear war in Europe?

By the time Margaret Thatcher came to office in 1979, tensions between the United States and the Soviet Union had reappeared. Détente was at an end, and the nuclear arms race was hotting up.

The year before Carter had increased US military spending by 3% in real terms – a necessary response, he said, to a build-up of Soviet forces during that decade. In 1980, Reagan won the presidential election on a Republican platform committed to 'restoring US military superiority'. Military muscle was also playing a more prominent role in Soviet foreign policy, most notable in the USSR's military intervention in Afghanistan in December 1979 – the first time Soviet combat troops were deployed outside the Warsaw Pact area since 1945.

In line with this changed international environment, the Tories' general election manifesto had identified the need to 'strengthen Britain's defences and work with our allies to protect our interests in an increasingly threatening world'. All NATO allies were under pressure from the United States to increase military spending, and in his budget statement the new Chancellor duly upped Britain's arms expenditure. As one defence minister told parliament, the government 'had no hesitation in endorsing the NATO aim of continued annual growth in national defence expenditure in the region of 3% per annum in real terms until 1986. We shall be taking this commitment fully into consideration when deciding future defence budget levels'. Defence was one area of public spending largely exempted from government cuts.

IRON LADY

Thatcher's central concern was the reorganisation of the British economy. She represented a break with the one-nation Conservatism of the Edward Heath era, seeking to replace post-war Keynesianism with a free-market approach to the economy. She identified with economic ideologues of the emerging neo-liberal era such as Milton Friedman, and appointed a prominent monetarist, Alan Walters as her chief economic advisor. Her foreign policy stance was belligerent – on the European Community as well as the Soviet Union, and on Argentina's claim to the Malvinas/Falkland Islands which she went to war over in April 1982. But contrast, for example, her response to the invasion of Afghanistan – encouraging British athletes to boycott the 1980 Moscow Olympics – with her acceptance of apartheid in South Africa. She stood out against Commonwealth and EC sanctions on the Botha government, and condemned Nelson Mandela and the African National Congress as terrorists.

Thatcher's approach on all matters military chimed with the orthodoxy of the Conservative right. Declassified government documents from December 1979 show no serious dissent in the Cabinet over plans to channel clandestine weapons to aid the Islamic opposition forces of the mujahidin in Afghanistan. Her attitude to security issues was conventional, framed in her many statements about protecting the 'British way of life'. She had already earned the 'Iron Lady' soubriquet in her first year as Tory leader, from a Soviet army journal reporting a speech in which she had focussed on the need to protect the British people from the Soviet threat. When the White House changed hands in 1981, Thatcher backed Reagan's ratcheting up of the Cold War. She shared his hard line anti-communism and commitment to strengthening nuclear forces. When Britain and the US reached an agreement to replace the Polaris fleet with American-leased Trident missiles, he was invited to address the

Houses of Parliament, only the second foreign premier ever to do so. He duly did so in June 1982, asserting that the Cold War was a struggle between the forces of good and evil, in which 'military strength was a prerequisite to peace'.

There were 50,000 nuclear bombs in the world when Thatcher took office, some of them up to 1,000 times more powerful than those dropped on Hiroshima and Nagasaki. The development of tactical nuclear weapons and proposed deployment of medium-range US missiles in Europe signalled that Pentagon planners were evaluating the possibility of theatre nuclear warfare – limited and potentially 'winnable' that is – as opposed to the conventional scenarios of the mutually assured destruction of the US and USSR in an intercontinental nuclear strike. The Soviet Union too was deploying its new SS-20 missiles in Eastern Europe. The possibility of nuclear war was back on the agenda, and a growing awareness of that was spreading across Europe. A re-work of the classic *Gone With the Wind* poster captured the mood of the peace movement – Thatcher in Reagan's arms superimposed over the image of a mushroom cloud, with the caption: 'The most explosive love story ever. She promised to follow him to the ends of the earth. He promised to organise it.'

LABOUR'S ALTERNATIVE

Labour's response was very different, especially on nuclear weapons. Concerns about nuclear war in Europe were addressed in its 1979 manifesto which stressed the need to 'strengthen world peace' and promised to 'work hard for disarmament'. The section on 'Détente and Defence' undertook that a Labour government would make no moves to build a Polaris successor or new generation of nuclear weapons, and promised to bring the UK's high arms spending down whilst protecting jobs. A Labour government would continue to support NATO, but the ultimate objective was the 'mutual and concurrent phasing-out' of NATO and the Warsaw Pact.

Labour's 1979 general election manifesto had committed a Labour government to:
– actively pursue a policy of détente,
– continue to work for the success of the Mutual Balanced Force Reduction Talks,
– give full support to the work of the United Nations Committee on Disarmament,
– work for the speedy conclusion of a Comprehensive Test Ban Treaty,
– give every encouragement to our American allies to achieve a successful conclusion to the vital Strategic Arms Limitation Talks,
– plan to bring the proportion of defence spending in line with European allies, and
– ensure savings in military expenditure did not lead to unemployment for those working in the defence industries, giving material support for industrial conversion so that the valuable resources of the defence industries can be used for the production of socially-needed goods.

On Polaris, the manifesto said: 'In 1974, we renounced any intention of moving towards the production of a new generation of nuclear weapons or a successor to the Polaris nuclear force; we reiterate our belief that this is the best course for Britain. But many great issues affecting our allies and the world are involved, and a new round of strategic arms limitation negotiations will soon begin. We think it is essential that there must be a full and informed debate about these issues in the country before the necessary decision is taken.'

After 1979, Thatcher's support for Reagan's Cold War policies, in particular the acceptance of US cruise missiles in Britain, signalled not only the possibility of a nuclear war in Europe, but one fought on UK territory. This brought opposition to nuclear weapons to the fore and strengthened Labour's commitments on nuclear disarmament. Spontaneous campaigns against cruise missiles sprang up supported by many local Labour Parties; and nuclear disarmers joined Labour, the party committed to get rid of them. Motions to the annual conferences of 1980, '81 and '82 called for unilateral nuclear disarmament by a Labour government, and were carried by big majorities.

CRUISE MISSILES

The Thatcher government formally announced the decision to allow US cruise missiles to be based on British soil in December 1979. Secretary of State for Defence Francis Pym told parliament that a NATO foreign ministers meeting had decided 'United States-owned and operated systems, comprising 108 Pershing II ballistic missile launchers... and 464 ground-launched cruise missiles' would be stationed in Europe by 1983. The British government 'fully supported' the decision because the missiles were 'essential if we are to avoid a dangerous gap emerging in NATO's theatre nuclear capability' which would 'cast doubt on the credibility of our deterrent capability'. In his term as Prime Minister Jim Callaghan had indicated his acceptance of US cruise missiles being based in Britain. But in the questions that followed Pym's December announcement, a number of Labour MPs voiced their doubts and attempted to tease out some of the undisclosed issues. Cost and control were major concerns.

The former was raised by Labour's Shadow Defence Secretary Bill Rodgers, who would split from the party a year later. Pym replied that infrastructure costs to the UK were calculated to be around £10 million. Ten days earlier, in a written answer, Pym had admitted that 90% of Britain's defence expenditure, representing approximately 4.25 % of gross domestic product, was devoted to 'forces deployed in the NATO area'. At a time of spending cuts and high unemployment, these extra demands on the public purse were significant.

Rodgers also raised US control, asking 'will there be any consultation process before the United States authorises their use?' Pym ducked out, saying only 'in so far as one can consult on a matter of national security, we shall certainly consult to the maximum possible extent'. But Labour backbencher Bob Cryer returned to the issue, asking him to 'confirm that only one key is involved in the use of these weapons' and if the use of one key indicated 'that the Americans have the right to enjoy the use of these weapons without consultation'. Pym's reply remained elusive: 'consultative processes that have been long established, which successive governments have thought to be adequate in all the circumstances'.

In his statement to the Commons Pym had asserted that NATO's decision was 'a dramatic reaffirmation of the American commitment to the defence of Europe... All 14 NATO countries concerned have agreed to support the programme'. In reality, support among European governments and their electorates was uneven. Germany, Italy, and Belgium, as well as the UK, had agreed to accommodate US missiles, but the Netherlands was still delaying taking a final decision, to which another Labour MP, Eric Heffer, drew attention. In private the British establishment was discussing a different picture to the one painted by Pym. A Chatham House paper at the time notes, for example, that the Atlantic Alliance was 'passing through a period in which its unity and cohesion are perceived as being under great strain', which was attributed to 'the apparent disunity among policy elites and the re-emergence of protest movements' in the context of a world recession.

In a Commons debate in January 1980, on siting US cruise missiles in Britain, Pym announced that the Polaris missile system would be upgraded at an estimated cost of £1,000 million. This was the first official acknowledgment that a missile development programme had taken place. Pym said: 'The previous Conservative government therefore pressed ahead with a programme of improvements to our Polaris missiles, which our immediate predecessors continued and sustained... the programme has now reached a stage where I can properly make public more information about it. The programme, which has the code-name Chevaline, is a very major and complex development of the missile [system]...funded and managed entirely by the United Kingdom with the full co-operation of the United States government, including the use of some of their facilities for trials and tests.'

Pym's statement revealed that Labour's manifesto had been less than honest about the Labour government's involvement with plans to upgrade the Polaris missile system. The government had called the debate on an adjournment motion (a formal proposal that MPs should go home for the night), and combined NATO 'modernisation', which Labour supported, with the upgrade of the missile system and a successor to the Polaris nuclear force, which the manifesto did not – a handy elision that helped the Labour leadership off the hook. Rodgers professed to be 'unfashionably agnostic' on Polaris, contenting himself with the mildest of rebukes, and wishing merely the debate had come earlier. The Labour leadership abstained on the vote, but a total of 54 MPs opposed the government, including 49 Labour MPs, almost 20% of the parliamentary party.

REPLACING POLARIS

In the January debate, Pym also indicated that a decision on a successor to the Polaris system would be taken soon. He estimated a 'total capital cost in the range of £4,000 million to £5,000 million at today's prices', spread over 10-15 years, which would absorb around 5% of the military budget. In a Commons statement in July, Pym announced that Polaris would be replaced by Trident:

'We have studied with great care possible systems to replace Polaris. We have concluded that the best and most cost-effective choice is the Trident submarine-launched ballistic missile system developed by the United States. President Carter has affirmed United States support for British retention of our strategic nuclear capability and United States willingness to help us in this...

'The agreement that we have reached is on the same lines as the 1962 Nassau agreement, under which we acquired Polaris. We shall design and build our own submarines and nuclear warheads here in the United Kingdom, and buy the Trident missile system, complete with its MIRV [multiple independently targetable reentry vehicle] capability, from the United States. Once bought, it will be entirely in our ownership and operational control, but we shall commit the whole force to NATO in the same way as the Polaris force is committed today. The new force will enter service in the early 1990s and will comprise four or five boats. We need not decide about a fifth boat for another two or three years, and we are leaving the option open meanwhile.'

Tam Dalyell objected, unsuccessfully, to 'such a momentous issue' being presented as 'a fait accompli to the House of Commons'. No vote was held on Pym's announcement, but five Labour MPs spoke to oppose the decision. 'Is it not time,' asked Robin Cook, 'that we admitted that we cannot go on providing the Alliance with the second largest navy, the second largest expeditionary force, and one of only two strategic nuclear deterrents formally committed to it? Will he at least come clean and tell the House what equipment he will now not be able to purchase as a result of this pathetic effort to pretend that we are still a super power?'

'Is it not clear that this £5 billion could be better spent on generating real industry in Britain and getting our people back to work,' said Eric Heffer, 'instead of creating a new series of nuclear weapons which, if they go off, from either side, can utterly destroy the world?' Bob Cryer described it as 'an outrage against humanity' and 'a completely corrupt set of priorities' given 'cuts in social services, education, school meals'. Stan Newens asked if Pym could 'envisage any circumstance in which the British nuclear deterrent might be used independently'; and Frank Allaun told him that 'the next Labour government may well cancel any contract that he enters into'.

In both January and July, the Callaghan-Rodgers leadership showed themselves to be lukewarm on Labour's manifesto commitments. Rodgers' response to Pym's July announcement that Trident would replace Polaris was just as weak as in January. The case for buying Trident has not been made and 'we cannot approve it', he said, and hoped for a full debate later.

GREENHAM

The announcement of when and where US cruise missiles would arrive in Britain had come a month earlier, in June 1980. Pym told parliament they would arrive in the UK in three years time, in 1983. The 'main operating base' would be RAF Greenham Common, in west Berkshire; additional missiles would be stored at RAF Molesworth, a disused Cambridgeshire airfield. This time round Pym put the total cost to Britain of NATO's modernisation programme at about £16 million – considerably up on the £10 million infrastructure figure he'd given parliament six months earlier in his December announcement.

Labour backbenchers again posed awkward questions: 'Would not the enemy destroy virtually the whole of Britain as a launching pad for the American missiles?' asked Frank Allaun. Were they not 'a distinct escalation of the arms race?' queried Bob Cryer; while Joan Lestor unsuccessfully sought an assurance that there would be no block on questions in parliament about the activities at the bases. Tam Dalyell re-visited dual key control: 'If the emphasis is on joint decision and if the Americans had meant it, why the reluctance to give us a dual key system?'

Joan Ruddock, a former chair of CND, had been Labour's parliamentary candidate in the safe Tory seat of Newbury in 1979, the parliamentary constituency in which RAF Greenham Common was located. She was returning home from work when the news of the missiles location broke. Her recollection captures the sense of urgency:

'When I got home I rang up the secretary of my Labour Party, Geoff Peppiat, and said we need to do something. We launched a campaign on the basis that it would be a non-party campaign. We set out the objectives – to oppose American cruise missiles on our soil – and agreed it over the phone. Geoff typed it up and delivered it to the *Newbury News* on the very night, and that was the start of everything. Two weeks later and nobody had taken much notice, so we wrote a letter to the *Guardian*. There was a huge response, absolutely huge response. And from there it just took off. That was to be the Newbury Campaign Against Cruise Missiles.'

Newbury Against Cruise, as it became known, was far from the only group of its kind. Similar campaigns began around the country. One such initiative began with a handful of women in Wales. Between 27 August and 5 September 1981 around 40 people, mostly women, walked over 100 miles from a nuclear warhead components factory in Cardiff to Greenham Common behind a banner that proclaimed 'Women's action for disarmament'. Dissatisfied with the lack of media attention their protest attracted, some decided to stay a while, establishing a temporary camp outside the gates of the base. The camp remained for 19 years. Greenham Common Women's Peace Camp became an international symbol of nuclear disarmament. As such it came under heavy attack from Thatcher and her ministers on more than one occasion as a hotbed of feminism and lesbianism – not much to distinguish between the two as far as many Conservatives were concerned.

Inspired by the women of Greenham Common, the non-violent direct action wing of the peace movement flourished. Led by the Fellowship of Reconciliation, a network of non-violent, religious activists, protestors set up a mixed women and men's camp at RAF Molesworth, where more cruise missiles were stationed. Like Greenham, Molesworth became a link in the

European anti-missiles network. Although hundreds of troops and police moved in to clear the camp in early 1985, protestors managed to hold demonstrations there over the next two years and a presence was maintained until the 1990s. In the three years from 1981 to 1984, the *New Statesman* chronicled protests and arrests at bases and other MoD facilities in Upper Heyford, Waddington, High Wycombe, Little Rissington, Boscombe Down, Porton Down, and Cottesmore.

WAR FEARS

Kate Hudson points out in her history of CND, that the only rationale for cruise deployment could be their potential use by NATO in a theatre nuclear war in Europe – an analysis 'borne out by the government's own glossy publication', which argued that 'smaller medium-range nuclear weapons' brought home 'to the Russians the appalling risks they would run if they pressed us further'. Nuclear strategists had begun to think the unthinkable: it was possible to fight a nuclear war and win. And the public knew it.

The magnitude of the anxiety this aroused can be seen in the exponential growth of CND. Membership shot up by 1,200% in the space of three short years – from 4,287 in 1979, to around 9,000 in 1980, 20,000 in 1981 and 50,000 in 1982. CND's local groups and affiliated organisations grew at the same sort of rate: from 150 groups and 274 affiliates in 1979 to around 1,000 each by 1982. On this one measure alone, we can begin to grasp the impact the arrival of the missiles had. CND held its first major demonstration of this period in October 1980. Tens of thousands marched across London to a rally that filled Trafalgar Square. In 1981 Hudson records that '16,000 protested in Sheffield; 10,000 went on a trans-Pennine march; 20,000 attended a march and rally in Clydeside; the Glastonbury Festival was run in aid of CND'. Demonstrations in London in October 1981 and 1982 each attracted in the region of a quarter of a million protestors. The biggest of these, in 1983, was estimated by the BBC to be 1 million people.

As CND's profile rose, so too did the attacks on the Campaign – testimony in practice to its political significance. Like the 1940-50s, much of the political debate was conducted on essentially dishonest terrain, including in the labour movement, with the same accusations that opponents of cruise were crypto-communists. In a contemporaneous account, Ruddock recalled: 'CND revived because people joined... One thing is certain – CND was not, as Frank Chapple suggested, "kissed back to life by the Kremlin"! On the contrary, western governments provided the stimuli.' Frank Chapple, general secretary of the electricians' union until 1984, was a poacher turned gamekeeper. A Communist Party member for almost 20 years, he then became one of the labour movement's most ardent witch hunters leading the charge to remove communist influence from the trade unions.

Right-wing organisations with Conservative Party links sprang up for the purpose of refuting CND. Michael Heseltine, Secretary of State for Defence from 1983 to 1988, established a CND rebuttal team in the Ministry of Defence. The Campaign, and the issue, took an all-round battering in the establishment's attempt to mobilise public opinion around support for a 'nuclear deterrent'. The organisations included the government-funded British Atlantic Committee, the Conservative Party's Campaign for Defence and Multilateral Disarmament, Women and Families for Defence founded by *Daily Express* journalist Lady Olga Maitland, and the Coalition for Peace Through Security. Thanks to the revelations of Cathy Massiter, the MI5 officer responsible for analysing CND telephone intercepts, we know that security service informants infiltrated CND. They found no hard evidence of communist links. Massiter has always maintained that her work was more to do with CND's political importance to the state than any threat of communist subversion. Ruddock, who was chair of CND from 1981 to 1985, recalls a barrage of such attacks:

'John Cox asked me if I would stand for chair. He said it was important that he was in a contested election because he was a member of the Communist Party. John was a major figure in CND and I certainly expected him to be elected. But to my utter amazement, I won. It had the most dramatic impact on my whole life. I was thrown into a maelstrom. I was besieged; my phone was tapped; and I nearly lost my job. It just got more and more intense as time went on, peaking in 1983 when the Consumer Affairs Minister threatened to remove the whole of the grant from the National Association of Citizens Advice Bureaux [her employers]. I had to work unbelievably hard. It was however thrilling, fulfilling, unbelievably frustrating at times, and sometimes quite frightening because of the challenges from the political establishment.

'CND was under attack from the government all the time. We were accused of taking money from the Russians and being spies for them – when Cathy Massiter gave her testimony, this was the reason that "justified" MI5's surveillance of me. They said I'd met a Russian agent posing as a journalist. CND never trusted anybody because we knew there were people everywhere trying to do us down. Whenever we did interviews we always ensured it was in a public place where we could be seen, and that we said the same things to everyone – the Russians, Chinese, Americans, the Brits, anybody. The message was always the same: opposition to *all* nuclear weapons. We never had anything to hide but it was so unpleasant at times, you had this sense you were being watched. And we had to accept that there was probably somebody planted within the CND office.

'CND was the broadest possible church – from anarchists to pacifists, people of the deepest religious beliefs to a few evangelical atheists like myself. It was the most extraordinary spectrum. They tried to make out we were all left wingers because we did have some Communist Party members. But the idea that you could run a disciplined, hard-left machine just wasn't realistic – and nobody wanted to.'

Julian Lewis MP, nowadays the Conservative chair of the Defence Select Committee, was working in the Coalition for Peace Through Security to expose what he believed to be the dangers of CND at the time:

'I met Brian Crozier in 1981, who had informal links with various odd branches of government at home and abroad. He said some of the people as it were on his bit of the spectrum were worried about the revival of the CND, and there were one or two groups who were getting up steam to try and counter it. One of them was the Coalition for Peace Through Security which was getting under way with my friend Edward Leigh and others. I thought it showed potential and therefore I decided to join forces with them. Edward was a former head of Mrs Thatcher's correspondence unit when she was leader of the opposition.

'I've always enjoyed campaigning. I am a conviction politician. The 1979 Conservative manifesto argued that the Western Alliance has kept our freedoms secure and the possession of nuclear weapons by both sides has been an effective deterrent to another war in Europe. This was, very considerably, a reflection of my own views. I think the fact that the superpowers did not take up arms against each other during the Cold War in any major way is a sign that the balance of terror is a deterrent. The problem with deterrence – and I readily acknowledge this – is that if it works it's always possible for the believer in nuclear disarmament to say that the peace would have been kept anyway.'

By 1992 Lewis was employed at Conservative Central Office, still the party's CND-attack dog. In the general election of that year, his rebuttal activities included compiling a dossier on the anti-nuclear sympathies of Labour prospective parliamentary candidates. *Labour's CND Cover-up* was published by Conservative Central Office on the eve of the election. It claimed that while CND counted between 100 and 130 Labour MPs as members, this information was unlisted in Labour's official directory of candidate biographies.

LABOUR'S DEBATE

By 1979 Labour was already a fractured party. Right and left vied for supremacy; differences of opinion on both sides were intemperately expressed. Many regarded the rise of the left as a temporary aberration, and after his defeat in the general election Jim Callaghan held on to the leadership hoping to halt the shift to the left. But the party moved left regardless, as conference voted for nuclear disarmament, withdrawal from the European Community, and perhaps most controversial of all, a process of automatic reselection of MPs. These policies represented the views of trade unionists as well as individual members. Without union support, there would have been no conference majorities.

This shift in party policy was not so much a dramatic about-turn as the culmination of dissatisfactions during the 1970s, especially over Labour government responses to upheavals in the international economy. Unhappiness over Labour government economic performance – particularly the 1978–9 winter of discontent which saw widespread strikes by public sector unions resisting expenditure cuts and Callaghan's 5% ceiling on their pay rises – was the background to the party's reaction to the first round of Thatcher's attacks. Many unions moved to the left in an attempt to defend members' jobs and living standards. Labour conference votes of 1979-83 were cast in this context.

Party members and trade unionists felt the same sense of

unease as everyone else over the threat of war in Europe; and a further concern was the rising cost of Britain's military spending which would knock chunks out of government spending on domestic priorities. Opposition was strongest on the question of US missiles in Britain. But unease went deeper. Perceptions about security – not always a high priority at election time – were also changing. Disunity among policy-makers in parts of Europe combined with the re-emergence of peace protests to highlight strains within the Atlantic Alliance. And after a period of reduced East-West tension in the early '70s, people were more ready to question the nature and extent of the Soviet threat, and the consequences of relying on the United States for Europe's security. For example, 33% of those sampled by Gallup in 1977 thought the coming year would be 'troubled with much international discord' and 33% thought it would be peaceful. Two years later, in 1979, 69% per cent thought the world would be troubled in the coming year, compared to a mere 7% who thought it would be peaceful.

Rodney Bickerstaffe, general secretary of the union leading many of the strikes at that time, NUPE, expressed his own view in strong terms:

'Personally, I've never, never wanted nuclear weapons. There are a number of arguments: the moral argument – I've been to Japan – and the fact that we're not going to use them. I can't imagine there was a moment in my life when I didn't say even if we've got that bomb we'll never use it. Who would in their right minds? Another argument is the amount of money that's spent when we've got people here and abroad dying of starvation. About 25 thousand old people die every winter in Britain from cold related illness... with some of that money you might be able to save lives. And what about that big old mushroom cloud, the inability to control where that goes – the environmental issues? They say the bomb's kept the peace, but does it stop war?'

He believes his views reflected those of his members:

> 'By and large I would argue that the rank and file, most of
> them, would not disagree with the things I say. Thirty five
> years with the union puts you in a position where you had
> to listen.... So when I spoke on platforms, on the radio and
> on television, I hoped that what I was supporting publicly
> is what the members thought.'

Not all unions supported nuclear disarmament, and the
core of support in the Labour Party for cruise and Polaris replacement came from the unions – the boilermakers (it became the GMB in 1982 after a series of mergers with smaller
unions), the electricians, the engineers, and the iron and steel
workers' confederation. Year after year, it was their members
who picketed conference delegates as they entered the hall
to vote, and who organised pro-nuclear fringe meetings with
Lady Olga Maitland and other such speakers. The GMB was a
fierce opponent of nuclear disarmament, despite representing
manual workers in local government, schools, health care and
other parts of the public sector that would be hit by hikes in the
military budget. It also represented members in the defence industry, some of whom worked on the nuclear submarines. John
Edmonds, a former general secretary recalls it as 'an enormous
issue that divided the TUC each year' but argues the GMB's position was firmly rooted in notions of trade union solidarity:

> 'You don't make other people redundant. That was really
> what it was about. In a sense whatever the political prin-
> ciples involved you got a free pass – everybody thought
> we've got to support those in ship building and defence.
> So there was some ambiguity about [the GMB's] position.
> Frankly, the T&G had a more difficult position: they had a
> stronger position against nuclear disarmament but they
> gave a free pass to their defence people. The desire to

keep people in work trumps everything.

'And they were good jobs in terms of skills, in terms of pay, in terms of quality of work, in terms of personal autonomy. The union had a lot of people who were in wretched jobs and these were much, much better. So it wasn't just a question of putting jobs at risk, it was putting quality jobs at risk. Always that argument was there. Even those people in the union – and there were quite a few – who were strongly in support of CND would say yeah, well of course they're going to defend their people's jobs. On the wider political issue fine, but on that basis there was no point in arguing because they were going to win it.'

1983 ELECTION

Labour fought the general election of 1983 on a nuclear disarmament platform. Motions to the annual conferences of 1980, '81, and '82 called for unilateral nuclear disarmament by a Labour government, and were carried by big majorities. Backed by over 70% of conference, this commitment now had the right to be included in Labour's election manifesto. Michael Foot, a leader from the centre left of the party and a founder member of the Campaign for Nuclear Disarmament, led Labour into the 1983 election. His foreword to the manifesto highlighted his commitment 'to help stop the nuclear arms race'. The manifesto undertook that a Labour government would:

– support the UN's 'call for a freeze on the production, deployment and testing of nuclear weapons' which the Thatcher government had voted against;
– 'not permit the siting of cruise missiles in this country' and 'remove any that are already in place'; and
– 'cancel the Trident programme'.

Jeremy Corbyn was elected to parliament for the first time in 1983. He recalls:

'I was very active in the party... [in] opposition to the Tory spending cuts. I was an official of the National Union of Public Employees, a councillor in Haringey, and election agent for Hornsey Labour Party. I was selected as parliamentary candidate for Islington North in 1982, a party with overwhelming support for CND. I made it a feature of this in the election campaign which we won with a 5,000 majority...Labour's commitment to nuclear disarmament affected the election in two ways: it mobilised CND supporters with hundreds of people helping, and it sharpened the election.'

His experience in Islington is borne out by accounts of what was happening elsewhere. Many party members believed the Thatcher government was too unpopular to survive the election. But party opinion differed over how to respond to the government's austerity policies and attacks on trade union rights, as well as US nuclear missiles. Labour was divided, not only on cruise, but on how to respond to Thatcher's first round of austerity measures, as the aftermath of the 1983 general election was to demonstrate.

In practice, the nuclear disarmament policy of conference and the manifesto was contested by senior Labour figures who made this crystal clear during the election campaign itself by speaking out against the policy. Two decades later, Labour's nuclear weapons lobby still argues unilateralism lost Labour the election. More dispassionate observers attribute the 1983 defeat to a number of causes, not least a split to the right by Labour's own Gang of Four, which are investigated in the following chapter.

CHAPTER 4

Labour's retreat

When US cruise missiles arrived in Britain, there were a total of 171 UN-recognised, independent states in the world, and a few other *de facto* ones. Only nine of them possessed nuclear weapons: the US, UK, Soviet Union, China, France, South Africa, Israel, India, and Pakistan. The latter four were not signatories to the nuclear Non-Proliferation Treaty which came into force in 1970; and Israel, India and Pakistan still are not. Israel didn't even admit to having nuclear weapons – and still doesn't to this very day, 60 years after testing its first bomb. Nowadays most of us know that Israel is nuclear armed because Mordechai Vanunu, an Israeli nuclear technician, told the world about them three years later, in 1986 – an act of bravery which earned him 16 years in an Israeli prison for treason and espionage, most of them in solitary confinement.

South Africa is likely to be the most surprising name on that list. Unless you've an especially good memory or a particular interest in the history of nuclear weapons, most likely you're unaware South Africa developed them in the 1970s and '80s, with the help of Israel; or that the UN Security Council introduced a mandatory arms embargo requiring all states to refrain from 'any co-operation with South Africa in the manufacture and development of nuclear weapons'. In 1989 President FW de Klerk declared that South Africa would end its nuclear weapons programme and dismantle its bombs. (It is sometimes suggested that the National Party saw the writing on apartheid's wall and didn't want a majority black country to have the bomb.)

South Africa is not the only country to have renounced nuclear weapons. Ukraine, Belarus and Kazakhstan have also given them up, although in very different circumstances. Each of these states had part of the Soviet arsenal sited on their territory when they became independent states. Indeed, the majority of states are covered by nuclear weapons free zone agreements that ban the use, development, or deployment of nuclear weapons in a given area, similar in purpose to the NPT, and in some cases covering nuclear power, waste, and propulsion too.

Possession of nuclear weapons is the exception not the rule, though you'd never have guessed it from the way the British political establishment reacted to Labour's 1983 general election manifesto. This wasn't simply a matter of one party's attempted hay-making at the expense of an opponent, though that was a significant element in the rumpus of course. Britain is exceptional in a second respect too, that of having a party of government that was prepared to end the UK's nuclear status. It was the latter more than the former which scared the pants off Britain's nuclear allies. Then as now, nobody with any knowledge of the subject seriously believed that getting rid of the UK's nuclear arsenal would significantly affect NATO capabilities. But it would have set a powerful precedent, and driven forward the demand for the global elimination of nuclear weapons.

Then as now too, there were a few senior military figures prepared to speak out against Britain's nuclear weapons. Field Marshal Lord Carver, who'd been the head of the British Army and Chief of the Defence Staff, was one. He argued that having a UK nuclear programme was inefficient when the US nuclear strike capability was powerful enough for everyone. When he died in December 2001, the *Telegraph* obituary commented: 'One of Carver's more blistering attacks was on the policy of nuclear deterrence, which he described as being either bluff or suicide.... The Trident missile programme seemed to him to be a waste of money and manpower which could have been better utilised on conventional arms...[and] when the communist regime in Eastern Europe collapsed he was critical of the plan to expand NATO...'

THE 1983 ELECTION

With favourable results for the Tories in the May 1983 local elections and Thatcher riding high in the polls, she called a general election in June. The economy was doing somewhat better than when she came to office, and the Conservatives were given a boost by their recent military victory over Argentina. The Tory manifesto emphasised employment, economic progress, and defence, including an independent nuclear weapons system. It remained committed to membership of the European Community, and promised trade union reform, further privatisation, and a long-term reduction in taxation. The Labour manifesto, in contrast, included withdrawal from the Common Market as well as the cancellation of Trident and the removal of cruise missiles from Britain. It promised an end to Thatcher's sale of council houses and an increase in public spending which would mean 'some taxes will have to be increased, both to shift the tax balance towards those who can best afford to pay, and to help finance our social programme'.

Thatcher's victory was decisive. Although the Conservatives' share of the vote dropped 1.5 points on 1979, from 43.9% to 42.4%, they increased their seats by 37. With 397 MPs compared to Labour's 209, Thatcher now had a whacking Commons majority of 144. The election result was widely recognised to be a disaster for Labour. Some described it as the party's worst election since 1918, others since 1931. Labour received only 27.6% of votes cast – 14.8 points behind Thatcher and down 9.3% on the 1979 result – and suffered a net loss of 51 seats, including Tony Benn and Joan Lestor on the left of the party. A total of 23 Social Democratic Party candidates also lost their seats – including Shirley Williams and Bill Rodgers, half of the Gang of Four which had split from the Labour Party in 1981, over differences on nuclear disarmament, the Common Market and greater enfranchisement of the membership. But the Lib-Dem-SDP Alliance finished only 2.2% behind Labour, winning 23 seats in all, 12 more than the LibDems held in 1979. Their support quickly declined thereafter, but at the time they were built up in the media as a rival second party.

Three days after the election, Foot announced he was standing down as Labour leader. In the leadership contest that followed, Neil Kinnock, who had risen to prominence as a supporter of CND, won an outright majority over his rivals in all three electoral colleges – Constituency Labour Parties, trade unions and other affiliates, and the Parliamentary Labour Party. His challengers were the right-wing former Foreign Secretary, Roy Hattersley, who went on to win the deputy leadership against Michael Meacher; Eric Heffer, the left's candidate; and Peter Shore, also a government minister in the 1970s and Michael Foot's shadow chancellor, best known as an anti-Marketeer. Heffer was the only one of these three opposed to nuclear weapons.

LABOUR'S CAMPAIGN

With cruise missiles about to arrive in Britain, nuclear weapons were a high-profile issue throughout 1983. A succession of opinion polls showed a clear majority against having US cruise missiles in Britain, and protests were stepped up, led by the Greenham Common Women's Peace Camp. The previous year had closed with an Embrace the Base action on 12 December, when over 30,000 women encircled Greenham airbase bringing down parts of the fence. In January dozens of women climbed over the fence to dance on the missile silos; hundreds entered the base again and again in February and March; and a joint action with CND in April saw 70,000 form a 14-mile long human chain that linked AWE Burghfield and Aldermaston, the UK's bomb making facilities, with Greenham Common, and protest actions continued over the summer and into autumn. In November, a fortnight before the missiles were to arrive, Michael Heseltine who had become Secretary of State for Defence at the beginning of that year told the House of Commons that 'intruders' on the base would run the risk of being shot. Undaunted, 50,000 women encircled the base again in December, tearing down parts of the fence leading to hundreds of arrests.

Whilst opposition to US cruise missiles was high and enduring, opinion on the broader issue of getting rid of Britain's nuclear weapons was more finely balanced and largely depended on how questions were framed. A question of the sort 'do you think Britain should keep its nuclear weapons to protect us from attack by the Soviets?' tended to elicit a majority yes response; whilst questions which favoured peace and conflict motion, or included public spending priorities also tended to elicit a yes majority. The first and most obvious lesson here is that nuclear weapons policy requires discussion and explanation. Labour's policies had to be elaborated and argued for. Reaching a wider audience was undoubtedly made more difficult because the political establishment and the majority of the mainstream media were hostile. But many believed that Labour failed to deploy all the resources at its disposal – including the weight of public opinion – because of the opposition at the top of the party.

Julian Lewis MP, nowadays chair of the Defence Select Committee, was an activist at the time, urging the Tories to take a hard line against nuclear disarmament. He explains how a parallel debate was playing out in the Conservative Party. Lewis and his colleagues were arguing:

'to go in hard and attack CND, and say they were too much under the influence of the left. Some MPs thought we shouldn't, by attacking them you're giving them more publicity. Our attitude was the exact opposite...

'Our target was the Conservative Party; our message was don't be fooled by the size of the demonstrations in

the street. These people are not going to vote Conservative anyway. And therefore do not be intimidated by the
noise that the CND is making.'

Lewis justified his approach thus:

'the purpose of effective propaganda is not usually so
much to change people's minds as to find out what they
think already and to reinforce it... And if it so happens
that you are campaigning on an issue where you've got
reason to believe two thirds of the British people wanted
us to keep nuclear weapons as long as the Soviet Union or
other countries had them... it's rather silly trying to ap-
pease the very small number of undecided people.

'I must be honest and say that the Conservative Party
in its campaigning on this issue should not be trying to
persuade people to come over to our side. They should be
appealing to the silent majority that we were convinced
was out there.'

Labour failed to take the same lessons on board, or perhaps
even to understand them. When it came to controversial or di-
visive issues, Labour spokespeople all too frequently wanted to
duck the issue – hoping to appeal to that section of the electorate least likely to vote Labour, and failing to reaffirm the views
of their own supporters. Even today, on issues which represent
a fundamental divide between the two parties, Labour still and
all too often attempts to direct its messages to those voters least
likely ever to back Labour.

But the Labour right were playing to an entirely different
gallery in 1983, just as they are today on Trident – seeking to
reassure the establishment that they too bought into the same
pro-nuclear club. Throughout the course of the '83 election
senior Labour figures attacked party policy. Under the headline
'Callaghan defends deterrent', *The Times* carried a front page

report of Labour's former prime minister saying: 'The Soviet Union's propaganda clearly wishes to use public opinion in this country to get the West to reduce its own arms while doing nothing themselves. In this way they would gain nuclear superiority. This is simply not on.'

Barely a week into the campaign, Labour's deputy leader Denis Healey told BBC *Newsnight* that Britain should only get rid of its nuclear weapons if the USSR made 'adequate concessions'. He was later reported by *The Times* as saying: 'We will put Polaris into the arms talks with the Soviet Union and hope to phase it out in multilateral negotiations... if the Russians... fail to cut their nuclear forces accordingly it would be a new situation that we could consider at that time.' Len Scott, an Aberystwyth University academic who was political adviser to Healey between 1984 and 1988, argues that behind the scenes his boss had persuaded Foot to include Polaris in future disarmament negotiations. Scott admits though that during the election Foot and his deputy appeared to disagree over the issue.

POLICY SHIFTS

Despite the election result, opposition to nuclear weapons among Labour Party members remained high and the conference that autumn reaffirmed policy – though a few of the more prominent advocates were beginning to show signs of cold feet. Labour CND and Labour Action for Peace, front runners in promoting nuclear disarmament policy, encouraged constituencies and affiliates to submit conference motions reiterating the commitment of previous years. Yet again the membership came up trumps. But Walter Wolfgang described what was happening behind the scenes meanwhile:

> 'The Labour leadership tried to persuade the delegates who were putting the resolution forward to let the matter drop by agreeing to refer the resolution to the National Executive Committee rather than having it voted

on it. Delegates refused this attempt to kick it into the long grass. When the NEC met reference back was also opposed by Eric Heffer, who was chair of the Labour Party that year. So it wasn't pursued further.

'I wrote a report about what was going on for *Labour Briefing*, one of the daily news-sheets published during annual conference by pressure groups in the Labour Party. We wanted to alert delegates, and harden their resolve. The resolution got debated and the unilateralist policy was reaffirmed again. We had the support of the majority of local party delegates and some of the unions, notably the transport workers, the fire fighters, and others.

'Some of the CND leadership were at the Labour Party conference and dissociated themselves from the Labour CND campaign to have the issue debated, and all hell broke loose. They created the impression that CND didn't support unilateral nuclear disarmament, and Labour CND sought to counteract this. So after the conference CND decided to "reorganise" its specialist section. The executive committee of Labour CND, which was democratically elected every year, was suspended and an interim one appointed by CND. Our rules were changed, and a special conference called to reconstitute us. But our opponents had badly misjudged the situation.

'Changing Labour CND's rules to give constituency parties more of a say by giving them more delegates and more votes was no threat as far as we were concerned. We knew our main support came from the local parties and we were confident that opposition was confined to a few, albeit vociferous individuals. They were hoisted on their own petard. When the special Labour CND conference took place, delegates from the constituencies overwhelmingly supported unilateralism. Our secretary Joy Hurcombe was re-elected as was I and other members of the disbanded Labour CND executive. Animosity continued for a bit after that, but CND's ruling council were solidly behind unilateralism too, and Labour CND continued to put it forward.'

Annual conference decisions notwithstanding, Labour's new leader set about finding some common ground with the party's Atlanticist right wing. Labour had never come near to having a majority of members opposed to Britain's NATO membership, and everyone knew it. Conference motions at the time, calling for the mutual dissolution of NATO and the Warsaw Pact, only picked up a few percent of the total vote and had no trade union support. Kinnock emphasised his willingness to work with NATO, stressed collective European security, and made clear he was as strong as Thatcher on national security. As events were to show, this was not so much an accommodation as the beginning of a capitulation. There were no serious attempts on Labour's part to utilise the majority support it had among the public to move the debate on, or prevent opponents within the party from speaking against the policy in public.

The first fruit of the leadership shift came in the form of a long document put before Labour conference in 1984, *Defence and Security for Britain*. Presented as an NEC statement, it had been drafted largely by Mike Gapes, a researcher in the party's international department who later became an MP. It reiterated support for non-nuclear defence, cancelling Trident and getting rid of cruise. But the emphasis was placed on Labour's loyalty to NATO and commitment to strengthening conventional defences. Conference passed it with a big majority; but delegates also voted to reaffirm nuclear disarmament, supporting motions on the same lines as previous conferences.

Over the next few years, NEC documents and statements took precedence over motions, until by the early 1990s the leadership felt perfectly comfortable appearing before the media to denounce conference decisions to cancel Trident or cut defence spending. In 1986, for example, with public opinion against the use of RAF Lakenheath and Upper Heyford for a US bombing raid on Libya by F-111 aircraft, Labour opposed Thatcher's decision to permit access to British bases. *Defence and Security for Britain*'s commitment to removal of US bases included F-111s; but in a TV interview, Kinnock argued there was no reason for removing F-111s because they had uses other than carrying nuclear bombs.

ELECTION POST MORTEM

Labour's post mortem on the 1983 election result began in the immediate aftermath of defeat, with the right pushing nuclear disarmament as one of the chief reasons for defeat. Corbyn recalls:

> 'I think nuclear disarmament was a positive as much as a negative for Labour. But it was played out frequently in debates in the House by some of the Labour right, those around Denis Healey. Neil Kinnock came and spoke at the enormous CND rally in Hyde Park in September 1983 as leader of the Labour Party. He said we don't need cruise, we don't need Trident, but Polaris should be put on the negotiating table.'

Though a small coterie of outspoken Atlanticists were courted and quoted by the media, inside the party there was little support for the view that nuclear disarmament had lost Labour the election. Nick Brown for example, a chief whip in the Tony Blair and Gordon Brown governments who describes himself as 'a pretty traditional Labour figure', trade union-backed and mainstream, is emphatic in a view which was shared by many in the party:

> 'The issue that is singled out for criticism in retrospect is nuclear disarmament. And I do *not* think that this was the issue that cost Labour the election... It was a whole range

of things. But the largest single factor – overwhelmingly in my opinion – was the Falklands War. The country had come together; there was broad approval of the stance that the Thatcher government took.'

John Edmonds likewise argues:

'What's the lesson from the '83 election? Don't fight an election when the other side claims to have won a war! It was all about the Falklands, triumphalist rubbish. The circumstances were unusual, very, very particular...

'The split and the formation of the Social Democrats was debilitating; organisationally we were a mess – but to say it was to do with nuclear disarmament? Well no, it wasn't... The SDP didn't get too many seats but they took a lot of votes away, that's absolutely crucial in a first past the post election.'

ORIGINS OF NEW LABOUR

Meanwhile, an intense debate opened up in top Labour circles. What had gone wrong, and how to fix it? In 1985 Kinnock appointed Peter Mandelson as Labour's director of communications, who in turn recruited Philip Gould, as a polling advisor. Both were to become key figures in Blair's New Labour team. From the start, they were out of line with Labour's mainstream. Walter Wolfgang offers a thoughtful, longer-term perspective of what was taking place:

'Keynesianism and neo-liberalism were in conflict by the end of the 1970s and by the '80s neoliberals were beginning to make inroads in the Labour Party. There was a strong tendency on the part of Jim Callaghan and the right of the party to embrace neo-liberalism, which ultimately resulted in the election of Tony Blair. By the time Blair was elected to the National Executive he was committed to neo-liberalism; he never had any time for Labour values.

'Thatcher wholly embraced neo-liberalism. In 1983 the British electorate felt the possibilities of neo-liberalism hadn't been fully realised, and were more likely to be realised under the Tories because the Labour commitment was half hearted.

'Neil Kinnock had reservations, but also embraced neo-liberalism to a large extent... It was felt that an anti-nuclear policy didn't fit with this changing approach. The United States, the home of neo-liberalism, would be hostile. Therefore Kinnock modified Labour's non-nuclear policy in the '80s...

'We managed to retain the confidence of the Labour Party conference for a long while; and while conference still had some power it was pushing in the direction of nuclear disarmament. Until Blair, after which democracy in the Labour Party was destroyed – not modified but destroyed by Tony Blair.'

From the start, Mandelson and Gould were out of line with the Labour mainstream. Reagan and Gorbachev were meeting for historic talks on reducing their nuclear arsenals, UK public opinion was clearly against cruise missiles, and successive Labour conferences were reaffirming the decommissioning of Polaris, cancellation of Trident and removal of US nuclear weapons and bases. Mandelson dismissed Labour's nuclear disarmament policies, on the other hand, as 'fashionable left-wing totems'; and Gould thought a defence policy without nuclear weapons 'was incredible to anyone with any vestige of common sense'.

In contrast, Bruce Kent, who joined the Labour Party 'sometime in the early '70s' offers an observation of the membership:

'I think I was mainstream Labour at that stage. Nuclear disarmament was part of the policy. I've got a letter somewhere in my cellar from Neil Kinnock saying we'll never change our policy on nuclear weapons. Getting rid of nuclear weapons *was* mainstream. We knew... that the actual technique of disarmament was a matter of controversy, but the commitment to get on with doing something about it was very solid...

'The spectrum of Labour Party opinion has moved so far in my time that I find myself now somewhere on the far left, the far Christian left... [but] the kind of view I express about social justice and all the issues of nuclear disarmament, the United Nations and all that, I think are really central to the general opinion of party members. I hardly go anywhere talking about poverty and the scandal of arms expenditure globally that the audience isn't on my side. So I think that I still represent a mainstream amongst party members.'

John Edmonds, a Labour loyalist who became an outspoken critic of New Labour in the 2000s, was a member of Labour's National Campaign Committee. He recalls the sharp change of emphasis the Mandelson and Gould era brought:

'Peter Mandelson became the director of communications for the party. He was the election guru for the 1987 election, and the idea was developed that you win the election by winning 7% of the population – those in the middle: Sierra man and Worcester woman – and that you have to have policies that locate you where that 7% feel comfortable. I've always had difficulties with the theory, but it was given enormous importance.

'Kinnock said we had to be realistic on Europe and realistic on nuclear disarmament. Those were the two principles that he thought we ought to change policy on – in order to give that 7% a feeling of comfort, that we were the cosy party and not extremist. There was a certain amount of PR stuff – the rose replaced the spade and the pen [Labour Party logos – ed]. And there was the beginning of triangulation: you find where your opposition are and you put yourself closer to that 7% than they are.

'But – and this is the big organisational change which presaged so much that came after – we had to have central control of election organisation and the messages of the election. You couldn't have campaigners going off and talking about whatever part of the manifesto they thought would be interesting. And of course we had a central diary. By the '87 election I was general secretary [of the GMB]. We were key campaigners, and all sent to particular places with the message of the day – 'be happy' or whatever it was…. This was the world according to Peter Mandelson and Philip Gould.'

Discussions were not about how to win, says Edmonds, but how to beat the SDP into second place. And it was this desire to overturn a harsh neo-liberal regime that brought Labour Party loyalists on side, even those who continued to feel strongly about nuclear weapons. New Labour insisted their perspective was the one that offered hope of a return to government:

'There was no debate about trying to win the election. I bought into this entirely – it would have required several miracles working in close proximity to each other to get us close to an election victory. All the polls were showing we were not only going to get beaten, we were going to get a beating. And the SDP threat which was disruptive in 1983 was now much more formidable and taking away votes, and was really destroying any chances of winning. That was the realism….

'One of the things we got from the polling each day [were responses to] the questions 'what makes you feel more positive about the Labour Party, what makes you feel less positive?'. Neil Kinnock came up most days as less positive. There was one occasion when Gerald Kaufman did something really stupid and he got the 'what makes you feel less positive'. It became a matter of gallows humour, because Neil really wasn't doing well.'

Edmonds recalls:

'It was during this period, '83-7, that the idea 'we must just find a winning formula' began to be developed, which of course created the wave that Blair eventually rode in on. But that was fuelled by the trade union movement because of the attacks that were being made on us.'

According to plan, the 1987 general election saw Labour in second place and the SDP tide ebbing. The Alliance share of the vote dropped 2.8% with a 1 seat loss; Labour was up 3.2% with a net gain of 20 seats. The Tories lost 21 seats, but Labour remained more than 11 points behind in the poll. The electorate's love affair with Thatcher had lost its first bloom of youth. Depressingly though, New Labour's approach provided few opportunities for the party to capitalise on voter discontent.

LEADERS VS MEMBERS

From here on in, central control over the party crystallised. A series of organisational changes began at the end of the 1980s and continued into the new century systematically robbing constituencies, and to a lesser extent trade unions, of their already-limited influence over policy-making. Internal democracy was stripped down to its bare essentials. This retrenchment was clothed in the language of Orwell. The procedures which were to remove members' influence in the party were labelled *Partnership into Power*; the leadership promised the new processes would be double-plus-good at making sure every member had a say in policy-making.

Nuclear disarmament motions continued to be submitted and

passed by conference. But with Gorbachev's successful Intermediate Nuclear Forces initiative and big changes presaged in the Soviet bloc, Labour CND and Labour Action for Peace turned their attention to the need for cuts in Britain's inflated military budget.

Bruce Kent recalls his experience as a conference delegate in 1989, when policy motions could still be moved and voted on. He proposed a motion supported by several constituencies and trade unions calling for defence spending to be brought in line with that of other NATO allies. With the support of most trade unions, it won an overwhelming majority.

> 'It was a wonderful experience [and] taught me so much about the workings of the Labour Party... There was a resolution which I was to speak to, ideal for me because it was about cutting expenditure on war. How can we possibly support this further military expense when people were suffering because of social injustice?
>
> 'I remember being called. It was a really exciting moment. There was this packed room and I had a speech already written out. I suddenly felt this is not the moment for a written speech, so I let rip. And I got a very, very warm response from the people there which I was delighted with. I imagine partly because I was identified with CND.
>
> 'Afterwards I found myself standing next to Mandelson, and Mandelson was not at all happy because I was getting all this applause. He was looking quite sick, and after a second or two he pushed off somewhere else...
>
> 'I didn't quite realise at that stage that you could pass all the resolutions you like, but when it gets up to the top they can decide what to implement and what not to implement. I thought what I'd proposed with that overwhelming support was going to be in the manifesto. No way! It wasn't in the manifesto.'

The following year the majority of the 74 motions and amendments submitted on defence reaffirmed defence spending cuts. Many of them recalled the 1989 motion had achieved more than the two-thirds majority required to get in Labour's manifesto, and duly called for its inclusion. Others reiterated the need to scrap nuclear weapons, and many called for defence diversification to protect jobs.

In 1991, motions were more varied. Some focussed on the aftermath of the Gulf War, and some on the dissolution of the Soviet Union. In consequence the number of motions on nuclear disarmament and arms spending cuts dropped. In 1992, nuclear disarmament was narrowly defeated, by around 46 to 54%. It had taken 14 years – and considerable effort on the part of the leadership - to prise nuclear disarmament off the agenda. Constituencies continued to put forward motions calling for an end to the Trident programme, but in shrinking numbers, and soon the topic ceased to be debated at conference.

THE 1992 ELECTION

When the general election took place in April 1992, Labour's manifesto promised: 'As the party which took Britain into NATO, Labour will base its defence policies on UK membership of the alliance. We will provide whatever resources are needed for effective defence for our country, providing the necessary level of forces with the appropriate equipment and weapons.' It made a commitment to 'set up a Defence Diversification Agency to assist workers, communities and companies affected by change'. But with masterful ambiguity said of military spending: 'The agency will ensure that resources made available by reductions in defence spending – reductions already planned by the Conservative government – are used in the first instance for rebuilding and investing in our manufacturing base.'

Three months after the formal dissolution of the Soviet Union, neither Labour nor the Conservatives, now under the leadership of John Major, offered a coherent approach to the changed international situation. Conference continued to pass motions committed to cancelling the Trident programme, but the Labour leadership now felt confident about disregarding them and was openly in favour of a British bomb. The manifesto commitments were considerably changed – but not for the better. Labour's line was confused and confusing on the subject of nuclear weapons, with a somewhat overblown commitment to 'partner the United States in negotiating to reduce the world's stocks of nuclear weapons' whilst promising to 'retain Britain's nuclear capability, with the number of warheads no greater than the present total'.

The Tories were no clearer on the collapse of the USSR and reverted to type. The Conservative manifesto warned of the need to 'remain on guard', insisting with uncritical aplomb: 'Britain has always been strongly opposed to nuclear proliferation', whilst boasting 'We are the only party unambiguously committed to the preservation and modernisation of our independent nuclear deterrent'.

In the days when local Labour Parties were relatively free to decide on who would be their parliamentary candidate, Bruce Kent stood for Labour in Oxford and Abingdon West:

> 'I wanted to stand somewhere in order to show that nuclear policies of the sort I have would not lose votes. They went for me, I think, under the illusion that a kind of Bruce Kent popular vote would come along, which there wasn't. I got about the same number of votes as the chap before me and the person after me. But I didn't lose any votes. There wasn't any surge away from Labour because of Bruce Kent's views on nuclear weapons.'

With Thatcher gone, and Major in difficulties, Labour was starting to close the gap. The Tories lost a net 40 seats in 1992 and Labour had gained 41, though it remained 7 points behind. Kinnock had failed for the second time to lead Labour to victory and quickly stood down. He was replaced by John Smith in July, who was to die in office less than two years later. The leadership election was a 3-candidate contest: Tony Blair, Shadow Home Secretary, Margaret Beckett, Deputy Leader of the party, and John Prescott, Shadow Employment Secretary who became deputy leader in 2007. Blair was elected on the first round by an electoral college of constituencies, affiliates and the parliamentary party, each casting one-third of the total votes. Labour's next leadership contest was not to take place until 16 years later, in 2010. When Blair stood down in 2007, Gordon Brown took over, the only candidate in an uncontested election.

PARTY DEMOCRACY

Kinnock's leadership was characterised by a growing distance between leadership and membership. The leadership's main objectives were to remove the already limited authority of conference over the content of election manifestos and to reduce constituency parties influence over their MPs by circumscribing their input into the selection process. From its inception, the Labour Party had operated on what was essentially a federalist basis. Power was shared between the parliamentary party, the trade unions, and local Labour Parties which exercised a high degree of autonomy –determining their own manifestos for local elections, for example, and choosing which issues they would and/or would not campaign on.

Labour's procedural shifts begun under Kinnock were continued under Smith, preparing the ground for what was to become a major reorganisation under Blair's leadership. Early changes were facilitated by two media obsessions: trade union influence in the party, especially their bloc vote at conference; and so-called 'entryism' – infiltration by groups deemed to be hostile to Labour values. The high-profile expulsion of the Militant Tendency softened the ground for open season on individuals and campaigns which operated openly and within the rules of the party. (A second round of witch hunting reached new heights with the election of Corbyn in 2015, when members of CND, for example, were refused a party card on the grounds that they belonged to an organisation hostile to Labour!)

The notion of one-member-one-vote (OMOV) was mooted as the means of reigning in trade union power. The proposal was put to conference in 1991, and carried. But the requisite rule change was lost when MSF, the scientific union, changed its vote. It was not incorporated into Labour's rule book until passed by the 1992 conference. Edmonds was no fan of OMOV but, like the majority of trade union leaders, he was 'prepared to accept a new structure'. He outlines the debate over the role of the unions by the time Smith, a member of the GMB, took over as leader:

> 'John Smith is convinced that we've got to work out some new arrangements, which enable him to answer questions about the influence of the trade unions in Labour Party policy making... The questions were these. Will trade union members have a vote in the election of the Labour Party leader? We settled that: yes. What about the proportions of the votes at Labour Party conference? The collegiate idea was 50% [constituencies and affiliates each cast half of the total vote – ed].
>
> 'Then comes the question which I thought was trivial: do trade union members have a vote in the selection of candidates? They have a vote in the selection of leader, so you can hardly say they can't vote in the selection of candidates, I mean where's the logic in that? And John Smith initially was, I thought, entirely in favour of that – just had to find a way of doing it, all the nerdish stuff...
>
> 'But Blair, Brown and Mandelson can see the battle terrain they want disappearing, two-thirds of it already negotiated away. If they're going to have a really different Labour Party, appealing to that 7%, then this connection to the trade unions needs to be finessed – like, got rid of!

So Smith was put under enormous pressure and he gave way to it unfortunately.'

This view of Smith's position is shared by Rodney Bickerstaffe:

'We were generally against OMOV, and I was against it. We were one of the very last unions to shift, equivocal right up to the end. We had many discussions with [John] Prescott and Smith... And Smith said to me, as he said to others, there will be no further action on structures. It would be an end to constitutional change. And I believed him and my delegation believed him.'

Edmonds did favour a new way of making policy though, as did other trade union leaders:

'The idea worked out with Kinnock and with Smith was that you have policy commissions that produce ideas for conference. These are voted on at conference, they can be amended at conference, and this makes up the mainstream of Labour Party policy-making. So you have commissions, overseen by something which was much slimmer than the National Policy Forum because the commissions were important, not the NPF.

'You would have a two year policy-making cycle, and the outcome would go to conference and would be voted on and would be subject to amendment... I thought that was a very civilised way of making policy in a modern age. It meant that you had the battles at conference over the major issues, you didn't have battles over every bloody thing.'

Edmonds explained that under Blair's leadership events took a different turn:

'Conference was a mess... all the media interest was in where the rows were coming from [which] could be over something really trivial. You had to have a better and more measured system of policy making but – and this is the difference – you had to retain conference's authority to either enforce, or to amend, or to reject what the policy commissions had said... But once Blair captured the National Executive, immediately the nature of the conference changed. The authority of the conference just went, flushed out of the system.

'Eventually [Blair] had to give ground and he introduced the nonsense of contemporary resolutions and emergency resolutions – you'd have to be very nerdish to know the distinction. But the main thing was that whatever the policy commissions put forward – well it rapidly became the National Policy Forum rather than the commissions – cannot be amended. So you either reject everything or accept everything which is an absolute nonsense. That's no way to make policy on anything.'

The Campaign for Labour Party Democracy had promoted democratic reform within the party with considerable success since it was set up in 1975. It acted as a watchdog for members' interests and became a trusted port of call for party loyalists. Now new organisations sprang up, concerned about the changes, and joined forces with CLPD. Doubts were by no means confined to the left, as Ann Black, nowadays an NEC member, explains:

'I went to a meeting in Birmingham which I think was the second meeting of people who were forming this new group, Labour Reform in 1996 and I felt very much at home... I remembered the old Benn-Healey wars and I'd actually found them pretty unedifying on both sides. But these were people who were not previously on the left, but alarmed by the speed and direction that the party might be taking. Labour Reform wasn't trying to revisit Clause IV or undermine Tony Blair's election as leader, but keep to some principles. So I became involved.'

In 1998 conference motions were finally scrapped, and the National Policy Forum took over that role. Shortly after CLPD, Labour Reform, Labour Left Briefing and others got together to agree a slate which became the Centre Left Grassroots Alliance. Black again:

'Pretty much from the beginning it has been solely con-fined to an electoral pact. It was formed to avoid all the small groups on the left putting up their own candidates…The desire was to have a single slate which would oppose the single slate that Millbank [Labour Party HQ – ed] would be running – it's Progress rather than Mill-bank nowadays. We've never gone beyond an electoral alliance in terms of coordinating the NPF and NEC. We don't have pre-meetings. We tend to support each other, but not always.'

This fightback was late in coming, and Labour's landslide win in the 1997 election provided New Labour with the cred-ibility they needed to cement their grip – at least for the present – on the party faithful. For the moment, New Labour had got its way over nuclear disarmament, but by foul means not fair. The debate was to recur within the decade.

CHAPTER 5
The Trident controversy

Labour had been out of office for 18 years when Tony Blair led the party to a landslide victory in 1997. Labour won 418 seats, an overall majority of 179. It was up 8.8 points, to 43.2% of the vote on a turnout of 71.4%. The Tories lost a whopping 178 seats and dropped more than 11 points in the poll. The British public's romance with neo-liberalism was at an end. Or was it? Within weeks of taking office Blair introduced legislation to reduce single-parent benefits which resulted in an early rebellion at the end of the year when parliament voted it through. Jeremy Corbyn and 46 other Labour MPs opposed the government – including Alice Mahon, one of the leading campaigners for single-parent benefits, and two other ministerial advisors. And a further 100 or so Labour MPs abstained.

Blair had spoken admiringly about Thatcher. He continued many unpopular Tory policies and, in some areas of traditional Labour concern, he adopted a tough-love stance that made many supporters uneasy. The BBC's assessment of New Labour at the time of the election proved pretty accurate: 'Blair – a public school, Oxford-educated barrister – was no son of the left or the labour movement'; his priority was 'to strip away policies that he believed had lost the party the crucial support of the middle classes in 1992'; the 'modernisation' of the party had 'escalated to a degree not previously thought possible'.

Nuclear disarmament was one of those stripped-away policies. The idea of abandoning Britain's nuclear weapons was no longer getting a look in. In a pre-election interview Blair had confirmed yes, if he was prime minister he would be prepared to sanction the use of Britain's nuclear bombs. Labour's manifesto promised 'strong defence through NATO' and that a 'new Labour government will retain Trident'. Attempts to raise the issue at conference continued but under considerably more difficult circumstances. Overall though, the party mood was one of enormous relief – at last, a Labour government! Members understood some important policies had been dumped en route, but the majority was grateful to have Labour back in No 10.

The new vehicle for a direct input into policy, 'contemporary' resolutions, meant nuclear disarmament could only be broached if something significant happened during a short period in the summer – after the National Policy Forum had agreed its report to conference, in early to mid-July, and before conference met at the end of September. Year on year, contemporary resolutions on Trident were ruled out by the committee which organised conference business. On the rare occasions Trident resolutions did reach the agenda, they fell at the next hurdle. Only a handful of contemporary resolutions could be prioritised for debate, and needed overwhelming support to make it onto the floor of conference. In addition, after 9/11, concerns about security increasingly turned towards the wars in Afghanistan, the Middle East and North Africa.

TRIDENT REPLACEMENT

The bomb didn't get back on Britain's political agenda until December 2006, when the government published a white paper, *The future of the United Kingdom's nuclear deterrent*, recommending that Trident be replaced. By then New Labour had successfully fought two general elections but was losing ground: a little in 2001, down by 2.5% and six seats; big time in 2005, dropping 5.5% on 2001 and losing 47 more seats – the fruits of Blair's Iraq war and revelations that MPs across the parties were falsifying their expense claims.

Three days after the white paper was out, Blair announced

in the House of Commons his decision to 'maintain' Britain's nuclear weapons system, which he described as 'the ultimate insurance'. In reality, maintenance meant a substantial upgrade, a modernisation of Britain's nuclear weapons which is rightly seen as proliferation. Four new up-to-the-minute submarines would be built, the most expensive part of the entire nuclear kit, and some other high-cost components would be replaced and updated. The current submarines would need replacing by 2024, said Blair, at which point they were anticipated to have reached the end of their active life. He argued it would take 17 years to design, build and deploy new ones, so the first steps must begin right now. There would be a Commons vote in March 2007.

There are three component parts to Britain's nuclear weapons system, which takes its name from the Trident D5 missiles which are leased from the United States: the warheads which are the nuclear bombs; the missiles which are the means of delivering the bombs to their targets; and four Vanguard-class submarines which carry the missiles and warheads, sometimes referred to as 'the platform', at least one of which is on patrol 24/7. Each submarine carries an estimated eight missiles with up to five warheads each. That's 40 nuclear bombs per submarine, each with an explosive power equivalent to 100 kilotons or eight times that of the atom bomb dropped on Hiroshima.

In his statement to parliament, Blair also offered MPs an estimate of the design and manufacturing costs of the Trident upgrade. Around £15-20 billion over three decades, he said, approximately 3% of the MoD budget. Within a few years, it became evident that these figures grossly downplayed the costs involved. A report commissioned by CND in 2014 put the overall cost of the Trident upgrade at a cool £100 billion over its life time. The government had already upped Blair's original estimate to £26 billion to build new subs. In October 2015, the CND figure was revised upwards again to £183 billion, based on the answer to a parliamentary question from Conservative

MP Crispin Blunt, a Trident sceptic. By the time the next Trident vote took place in parliament, in July 2016, the government was estimating replacement cost at £31 billion – more than a 50% increase on its original figure of nine years earlier. CND's revised estimate was £205 billion total lifetime costs, based on government figures in the public domain.

Blair's announcement of a Trident replacement was far from popular. The TUC's then-General Secretary, Brendan Barber was among the first to call for the decision to be delayed. 'We need a much wider public debate about Britain's role in the world and the role that nuclear weapons play,' he said. 'We also need to consider the impact on government spending and on jobs and skills of a decision either way.' A few opinion polls were providing early evidence that Trident remained unpopular with the public, despite years of Tory scare-mongering and Labour's policy about-face. Two ICM polls in January 2007 showed 64% against having nuclear weapons based in Scotland, and 73% of Scots against the billions spent on replacement. Two months later, a Populus survey found 72% of respondents across Britain were opposed to government plans for replacement.

National Policy Forum member, Ann Black provides a flavour of the Labour mood in early 2007:

'The NPF had a meeting with Des Browne [Secretary of State for Defence] in February 2007. Deborah Gardner [an NPF member – ed] had done a survey of members, and more were against replacing Trident than for it. Though I think it was not top of people's list of what they were thinking about... And before Andrew Smith voted against the whip he had the people in his office do a little bit of calling round [in his constituency] to find out if voting against Trident would be unpopular with our core vote – not *Guardian* readers but council estate tenants. Apparently what they said was we trust you to make the right decision.'

During the parliamentary debate in March, Labour MP Mohammad Sarwar also reported: 'To date, I have not received a single letter in support of its replacement. That is a clear indication of the strength of public opinion in my home city of Glasgow and in Scotland against the replacement programme.' Unsurprisingly, Trident was least popular in Scotland among those living on its doorstep. Successive polls since then have also thrown up majorities against replacement across the whole of Britain. It was only after Corbyn's election in the autumn of 2015, when the combined onslaught of the Tories, the Labour right and the media was devoted to attacking his views on nuclear disarmament, that the opinion pollsters were able to produce a couple of results with small majorities supporting Trident.

LABOUR REBELLION

Blair's promised debate on Trident was held on 14 March 2007. With Conservative backing, he won the vote 409:161. There was a substantial Labour rebellion though – the biggest since the Iraq war debate in 2003, and the second most significant of Blair's premiership. Labour opposition included 16 former ministers, four of them ex-cabinet members. Four of the rebels were serving ministers in Blair's government at the time of the vote, and resigned to break the party whip: Labour's deputy leader of the Commons Nigel Griffiths, and three ministerial aides – Jim Devine, Stephen Pound, and Chris Ruane.

Speaking in the debate Griffiths said he had read the white paper and concluded that Trident 'has no future – that this country has to become a country for peace, not a country for war... we must lead the world in campaigning for the eradication of the nuclear threat – and we must lead by example'. He was 'overwhelmed by the messages of support I have received'.

Jim Devine also spoke, quoting at length from Blair's first Foreign Secretary, Robin Cook who had resigned from government in early 2003 over the impending invasion of Iraq. 'There could not be a more convincing way for Tony Blair to break from the past and to demonstrate that he is a true moderniser than by making the case that nuclear weapons now have no relevance to Britain's defences in the modern world... [but] the spirit of the Cold War lives on in the minds of those who cannot let go of fear and who need an enemy to buttress their own identity.' Devine also repeated Cook's reminder that 'all levels of the Trident system depend on US cooperation. The missiles are not even owned by us, but are leased from the Pentagon in an arrangement that Denis Healey once dubbed as "rent-a-rocket".'

An amendment from Labour MP Jon Trickett said the case for Trident replacement was not yet proven and the need for an early decision was unconvincing. It attracted the support of 101 Labour MPs (counting David Taylor a Labour teller). And when the government motion was put to the vote 92 voted outright against Trident replacement. During the six-hour debate in parliament, hundreds of protestors had rallied outside, joined by celebrities such as singer Annie Lennox, fashion designer Vivienne Westwood, and human rights activist Bianca Jagger. Using nuclear weapons would be 'the end of life as we know it', said Jagger. 'My belief in the moral sense of politicians has been really affected.'

Corbyn recalls:

> 'When the first vote took place on Trident in 2007, this led to a big parliamentary debate and a big campaign outside parliament by CND and its allies. One hundred Labour MPs voted against Trident replacement on a three-line whip, which was astonishing. The Conservatives supported Trident replacement and we then ended up with the initial decision which was that Trident should be replaced, and this has enabled the government to claim parliamentary approval for spending probably about £3 billion ahead of the main decision in 2016.'

He summarised the arguments put forward:

'The all-party front bench consensus on nuclear weapons has been broken by backbenchers on both sides. On the Labour side there's been those like me who adopt a traditional position if you like, of opposition to nuclear weapons; and on the Conservative side there are those who would use a military analytical position as to why nuclear weapons are irrelevant – that is, not wanted by the military, and also very expensive. So I think there's a combination of moral and practical arguments: that international security is not brought about by nuclear weapons, it's brought about by peace, understanding and equality; and that the military don't want to see an increasing proportion of a decreasing military budget taken up by nuclear weapons.'

Anticipating the announcement about a Trident replacement, Trickett who moved the opposition amendment, had sponsored Rethink Trident, a campaign against replacement in which CND worked together with War on Want, Compass, Pax Christi, Scientists for Global Responsibility and others.

CHANGE OF MOOD

Whilst opinion against nuclear weapons held up under New Labour hostility, both in the party and among the public, the issue did not generate the same level of grassroots activism it had in the 1980s when many believed the possibility of a nuclear war in Europe was looming. By the turn of the century, a new politically conscious generation had become acclimatised to the idea of nuclear weapons. Less aware of what happened in Hiroshima and Nagasaki, they had adjusted to the idea of the bomb being around. The threat of nuclear war was remote, the issue of nuclear disarmament less urgent.

This difference was expressed by Billy Hayes, general secretary of the Communication Workers Union from 1992 to 2015. Hayes himself has a strong commitment to nuclear disarmament, and the CWU had supported a nuclear disarmament policy for Labour for more than two decades, including helping found Rethink Trident when replacement was raised by Blair. But Hayes felt it was never a 'top priority' for his members:

> 'So sad to say, I don't think peace and nuclear disarmament is a big or active issue among members. It's not on everyone's lips that's for sure. The CWU moved the motion [reaffirming opposition to Trident replacement] at the [2013] TUC and it went through without opposition. It's starting to get there, but I'd be a liar if I said it was a big issue in our union, it's not.'

From the announcement in 2006 to the final vote 10 years later, the weight of evidence – from peace movement activities, from opinion sampling, from public debates, MPs' statements and questions, and discussions in local Labour Parties – all suggests that opposition to Trident has remained constant and high. But the crucial question – how to make it count? – is unresolved.

Corbyn offered his opinion that:

> 'There are some people in my constituency who are very conscious of Trident. And there is a much larger body of people who are engaged in trade justice networks, supporters of Oxfam, and so on; and an even wider grouping that would be loosely described as concerned about human rights. I get a huge correspondence on causes like that. But is Trident a big issue within the constituency? No. Some young people are almost unaware of what nuclear weapons are.
>
> 'I think the peace movement makes a mistake in referring to Trident all the time, which doesn't mean very much to many people. I think it should start referring to nuclear weapons or weapons of mass destruction which

has more purchase. I recall a discussion with a young family who couldn't understand why I was against the Met's Trident investigation of black on black gun crime. They'd never heard of Trident nuclear missiles... it was quite an education session.'

SHIFTING SANDS

The transition from Blair to Brown came three months after the Trident vote, in June 2007. Economic storm clouds were gathering, and some hoped Gordon Brown's leadership would see a deceleration of Britain's involvement in Middle East wars and perhaps Trident too. They were disappointed. Brown's base, strongest among the traditional trade union right in Scotland and elsewhere, was dyed-in-the-wool supporters of Britain's bomb with conventional views about maintaining Britain's world role via its place on the UN Security Council.

At the same time, the 2005 and 2010 elections saw some of Labour's most stalwart opponents of nuclear weapons step down – Alice Mahon in 2005, a long-time peace activist sickened by Blair's Middle East adventures; Gavin Strang, Ann Cryer, Neil Gerrard, Bob Marshall Andrews, Alan Simpson and other Trident opponents in 2010. They were replaced by a new generation of Labour parliamentarians with different political viewpoints and aspirations. Many of them had little connection with the nuclear weapons issue, and the same might be said, to a lesser degree, of a new generation of party members in the constituencies. Labour's defeat in the 2010 election and Ed Miliband's election as leader that autumn, coupled with important changes in Britain's political landscape did bring some small shifts on the Labour front bench however.

In 2010, with the final decision on Trident replacement looming, a hung parliament had resulted in a Conservative-led coalition with the Liberal Democrats. There were significant differences between the two on Trident replacement. There was an established opposition to nuclear weapons among the

LibDem membership which successive conferences had watered down but not got rid of, and opposition was reinforced by the recruitment of left-leaning new members joining the LibDems rather than New Labour. LibDem policy opposed 'like-for-like' Trident replacement, but not necessarily another nuclear weapons system. The LibDem leadership searched for a viable position to square the circle, and Cameron agreed that a review of alternatives could be conducted by the Cabinet Office. As a result, in July 2013, the government published its *Trident Alternatives Review*, stressing this was neither a statement of government policy nor an endorsement by the government of other possible approaches to 'deterrence'.

Deputy PM Nick Clegg insisted there were options other than like-for-like replacement, while Danny Alexander, a LibDem cabinet minister assured the media that the report showed other choices were possible. The LibDems were exploring options such as an alternative platform to the submarines, less of them on patrol, or not on patrol 24/7. At the same time, the SNP were drawing attention to an entirely different perspective, insisting that an independent Scotland would not accept Trident based in Faslane.

Cameron continued to stress the Conservative commitment to a round-the-clock submarine-based nuclear weapons system. The review came to nothing, the government position remained unchanged. The Labour front bench meanwhile, appeared to have read the writing on the wall at last. Nick Brown drew attention to the changing terminology of Miliband's team. The commitment in the 2010 Labour manifesto was to 'maintain our independent nuclear deterrent', whereas in 2013:

> 'The commitment is we will maintain the minimum credible nuclear deterrent. That is the current party commitment. The words that our front bench spokesmen now use include "minimum" and "credible". And the reason is to give enough room to respond to the review... [which

is] much discussed, and see the sort of ideas that are coming out...

'They haven't given their commitment to four new Trident platforms. Although the individual members of the defence team see the shortcomings of most of the alternative platforms – and on that, just on that point, I think they're right...'

Elected to parliament for the first time in 1983, Brown went along with the changes in Labour policy on Trident under Kinnock and Smith, and as chief whip during the Blair and Brown leaderships, he was an enforcer. When Miliband took over, Nick Brown ceased to be part of the front bench, and has since spoken out against Trident replacement – not from opposition to nuclear weapons *per se*, but from what might be termed a more pragmatic perspective:

'I accept membership of NATO, indeed I'm in favour of it... [and] believe that we should contribute to supplementing NATO's weapons rather than replicate one that we could never use independently of our NATO membership. The key question for me was to describe the circumstances in which Britain would independently use a strategic nuclear weapon and against whom. And nobody's got a satisfactory answer to that.'

In the 1980s:

'The question that faced the country, not just the Labour Party, was whether we would prolong the life of the Polaris... or buy a new platform, a completely new platform we now know as Trident, and put on it the next generation of nuclear armed missiles. That meant a deal with the Americans on the weapons system...

'The big issue under Mrs Thatcher's government was

to decide whether to buy the platform. The question for all subsequent governments was whether to keep it, and that is a different question. The money had been spent, or was being spent. The contracts couldn't be cancelled, or the penalty clauses would have been so severe that it was as expensive to cancel as to press on. So we were stuck with the thing for its lifetime.

'And I have to say most mainstream politicians acquiesced in that. It's not ideal but it's the price paid... that is why I feel so strongly about it now. This isn't about do you keep something you've already got. This is about do you build a new platform and saddle the next generation with 35 years of it. It won't be used – at least I can't conceive of the circumstances, not in my wildest imaginings, when we could use it for its stated purpose, independently.'

The difference now is:

'At the next general election, the electorate will be aware of the renewal of the Trident programme – do we want to buy this thing again for 35 years, to commit ourselves to a new platform that will last for that period of time?– and everyone will be asked where they stand. If the idea is just to push it to one side and hope that Labour don't have to answer that question, I think that's an error...

'I would say there's a substantial number of Labour MPs who would not be in favour of renewing. I can't speak for our candidates at the next election; I haven't canvassed the party so I don't know. But what I can say with confidence is that there is a division of opinion, some of it running quite deep. Remember the question is not do you acquiesce in a weapons system you've already got and paid for. The question is do you do it all over again?

'That is such a huge distinction, and public expenditure will be a big issue at the next election – debt, deficit, what the government can afford to spend. This is £100 billion you're committed to which is not a small sum of money. And it's not in the abstract either. If you do this, there are other things you cannot do.'

Joan Ruddock, who'd campaigned in the '80s and remained opposed to Trident, explained a different set of concerns at work among Labour MPs:

'I think quite a lot of people who have been supporters in the past would be quite ready to see Trident go. But they perceive the problem of an attack from the *Daily Mail*, and we know how damaged Neil's image was by attacks from the right wing media... There's a very great fear that if you give the Tories *anything* to hang you with, the noose will be on your neck, pulled by every right wing media. And the attacks in the Commons would be absolutely con- stant... it's just such an easy wicket because the Tories can get about 98% of their people roaring on this issue.'

Her comments, made in 2013, take on a prophetic quality in post-Brexit retrospect. In the turmoil that followed the EU ref- erendum result, Prime Minister Theresa May, in post a mere few days, led a debate in parliament which confirmed the decision to go ahead with Trident replacement. Cameron had delayed the decision until after the general election – another recogni- tion that popular opinion was not with replacement – and given the need to concentrate on his ill-starred referendum debate, it was widely anticipated that the Trident decision would take place in the autumn. But the vote was sprung on parliament in July – the timing clearly designed to divert attention away from warfare in the Tory Party by focussing on Labour divisions.

LABOUR'S DEFENCE REVIEW

Corbyn's election as leader and the conference decision to hold a review of defence policy had unleashed a much-needed debate in the party. For months, supporters and opponents of Trident had debated each other in Labour branches and constituencies across Britain. Ironically enough, Progress put John McTernan up as their main speaker for Britain's bomb, whose most recent incarnation was Chief of Staff, 2014-15, to Jim Murphy, Labour's Scottish leader and a former shadow defence secretary who had to stand down after the 2015 election. Not only did Murphy lose his own seat, but the dreadful duo's claim to fame was to see the party wiped out in Scotland, losing 40 seats to the SNP and leaving Ian Murray, Edinburgh South, as Labour's last man standing.

Local party debates on Trident were many and varied. CND-supporting speakers emphasised Trident's inability to protect Britain from real threats, its dependence on US know-how, and cost. Progress and Labour First tended to fall back on old themes from the 1980s – ramping up the dangers of Russian aggression and playing on members' fears of losing the next election – but never acknowledging what the use of a nuclear bomb would do or the circumstances in which it might be used. In one debate, a Labour First speaker began in typical fashion laying great stress on his personal revulsion at the idea of using nuclear weapons, and parading his Christian socialist credentials before arguing that Trident must be replaced!

Some local parties found imaginative ways of opening discussion up – like Horsham for example, where the party joined forces with the local college to hold a public debate addressed by students, academics and Labour Party members, attracting a big audience and a front page write-up in the local press; and Hastings, where contributions from speakers were kept to a minimum, in favour of break-out groups of members debating different aspects of the constituency's submission to Labour's defence review.

The announcement of another leadership election provoked by the mass resignation campaign by some shadow cabinet members meant the results of the defence policy review conducted by Emily Thornberry as shadow defence secretary were never made public. It was expected to be sceptical about Trident, and two parallel reviews had been called: one by the International Policy Commission, a tributary into the National Policy Commission's annual conference report; and another invitation-only review by John Woodcock, a notoriously pro-Trident MP who chairs the Parliamentary Labour Party's backbench defence committee. The IPC's deliberations were also halted by the close-down of the party which accompanied the leadership contest. But submissions were available on line. One hundred of them, out of a total of 130, were partly or entirely about nuclear weapons, and 67% of those opposed Trident. Online comments and votes on the submissions were even more strongly opposed.

The government's National Security Risk Assessment report of November 2015 identified the most likely and immediate threats to UK security to be terrorism, cyber-attack, instability in the Middle East and elsewhere, health pandemics, natural disasters, and the activities of transnational criminal gangs, such as people trafficking. It categorised the threat from weapons of mass destruction as a Tier 2 threat, more remote that is. And even in this case, the NSRA considered the likely scenarios for the use of WMD to be chemical or biological attacks against the UK mainland or British troops abroad. But despite this clear advice, the government used the Commons debate to try and persuade MPs that Trident was necessary to protect Britain and that the security nuclear weapons provided justified their high cost. The government's resolution even began by claiming: 'That this House supports the Government's assessment in the 2015 National Security Strategy and Strategic Defence and Security Review that the UK's independent minimum credible nuclear deterrent, based on a Continuous at

Sea Deterrence posture, will remain essential to the UK's security today as it has for over 60 years...'

With Labour's defence review unresolved, the PLP was free to vote as they chose. Many Trident supporters bent over backwards to support the Tories. No sooner was the PM on her feet than the Labour toadying began. John Woodcock reassured her that 'many of my colleagues will do the right thing for the long-term security of our nation and vote to complete the programme that we ourselves started in government'. Mike Gapes reminded her that 'the Labour government of Clement Attlee took the decision to have nuclear weapons'. Kevan Jones invited her to 'pay tribute to the men and women working in our defence industries' and agree 'it is vital for the national interest to keep these people employed'.

A FINAL DECISION?

It was a surprise to no-one that the government won the vote, and the media hailed it as a thumping majority. Less remarked on was the extent of the opposition. A total of 458 MPs voted for Trident replacement. But there were 117 votes against the government, and 52 abstentions – the majority of which are believed to be deliberate choices not to vote. Among Labour MPs, 140 voted for replacing Trident and 47 against, with 41 abstentions. There had been a campaign for abstentions within the PLP, on the grounds that the vote was unnecessary and called by the Tories to show divisions in Labour's ranks; it is likely that many of the 41 represented a deliberate choice not to cast a vote. They included Emily Thornberry, former defence secretary, and Clive Lewis, recently-appointed to that post, both known to be nuclear weapons sceptics.

An analysis of voting throws up two important aspects of the Trident debate. First, at least a quarter of MPs did not support the government. Second, opposition extends across the parties. All 56 Scottish National Party MPs voted against, as did Plaid Cymru, the LibDems, and the Green Party's sole MP, Caroline Lucas. One Conservative MP also voted against – Crispin Blunt, chair of the Foreign Affairs Select Committee. We may take this as another reflection of public opposition to Trident.

CND had already moved into a higher gear in anticipation of the final phase of the parliamentary discussion, calling a national demonstration in February with dozens of partner organisations in support. Nuclear disarmers took to the streets of the capital in the biggest turnout against nuclear weapons in a generation. Unaware of the timing of the impending debate, CND had also organised a mass lobby of parliament in July – as it happened, only five days before the government debate. Hundreds of people came to London to tell their MP what they thought. On the day of the vote a CND-organised petition of 40,000-plus signatures was delivered to the Ministry of Defence and that evening, as MPs deliberated Parliament Square filled with protestors, conjured forth at a few days' notice.

The vote in parliament does not represent an end to the Trident debate. Public opposition is far from exhausted. In some respects it is stronger than ever before. Labour's highly politicised debate notwithstanding, in the post-Cold War period public opposition to nuclear weapons is part of the mainstream. A substantial minority at least, perhaps even a majority now regard the bomb as a costly and anachronistic form of 'defence'. Regardless of the disappearance of Labour's ill-fated defence review, efforts to shed the party's nuclear disarmament 'baggage' are failing yet again.

CHAPTER 6

Back to the future?

After a summer of speculation, Jeremy Corbyn's re-election as Labour leader was announced at the party's 2016 conference. More than anything, his second victory was a testimony to the strength of feeling among Labour Party members and supporters that *Things Must Change*. Over half a million votes were cast and Corbyn had a clear majority – 58.98% of members votes; 69.88% of registered supporters; and 60.23% of affiliated supporters. Corbyn's victory is also a tribute to his staying power and that of his team. This is particularly ironic given the focus of attacks from his opponents was the claim that Corbyn is incapable of becoming prime minister. With the benefit of hindsight, his cool-headed determination under fire, and dignified response to some exceptionally personal criticism, ticked two big boxes for any prime ministerial candidate.

The same hindsight, by contrast, casts deep doubt on the strategy and tactics of the anti-Corbyn campaign. According to Owen Smith, his challenge stemmed from a belief that Corbyn didn't have what it takes to be prime minister. Smith ran a more-socialist-than-thou campaign (suggesting either that Corbyn's policies weren't the problem, or a cynical attempt to capture Corbyn votes). But Smith threw in the towel before the contest closed – an un-prime ministerial characteristic if ever there was one. Conceding he was unable to win by announcing his intention to return to the backbenches, he made the bizarre suggestion that he hadn't favoured an early challenge to Corbyn's leadership in the first place! Other Corbyn opponents were rethinking too. Before the results were in, 14 of the 20 MPs whose resignations from the shadow cabinet precipitated the leadership challenge also announced their willingness to return to Labour's front bench.

It's right, of course, for Corbyn to incorporate different opinions and expertise on his front bench. And second time round he does so from a position of greater strength.

MOOD CHANGE

Corbyn's improved status and renewed confidence was reflected in speeches and policy announcements – though nuclear disarmament was a significant exception. And delegates were pleased with the elaboration of Labour's policies – on the Tories' proposed reintroduction of grammar schools, on extra council borrowing to fund more council home building, on the commitment to an interventionist government and a 'real living wage', and on the promised removal of private provision in the NHS. Conference registered an unmistakable mood among party activists. They wanted an end to the internal warfare of the past year too, and Labour united ready for the next general election.

Sadly though, signs to the contrary emerged before conference even ended, including a change in NEC representation, shifting the political balance away from Corbyn, and continuing demands that neither the leadership nor the membership but the PLP alone elect the shadow cabinet. Deputy Leader Tom Watson led for the right on the floor of conference. Carefully crafted to undermine Corbyn, his speech was full of references like 'a Labour woman prime minister is long overdue', 'Labour in power, not just talking the talk', 'trashing our own record' by 'focusing on what was wrong with the Blair and Brown governments'. And Watson pushed a big anti-Corbyn button with 'capitalism, comrades, is not the enemy, money's not the problem'.

Old New Labour was up and running in front of the media too before conference closed. Mandelson called for an early election: 'Bring it on so we can deal with the awful situation in the Labour Party earlier than 2020'. But first-class honours in self-deception have to go to Tony Blair, who responded to Corbyn's re-election with the news that he was thinking about returning to frontline politics.

TRIDENT CONTROVERSY CONTINUES

Corbyn's advances notwithstanding, attempts to change policy on Trident fared poorly at Labour's 2016 conference. Trident motions didn't make it onto the agenda, there was a concerted attempt to kick Labour's defence review into the long grass, and the party shutdown during the leadership election meant members had had less opportunity than usual to influence the National Policy Forum's report to conference. The true state of party opinion was all but unrecognisable in the NPF statement on defence policy. After hearing 'expert evidence' and noting the 'many submissions from members, CLPs and others... including on... nuclear deterrence', the report came down firmly on the side of Trident.

Maintaining silence on the incomplete defence review, Clive Lewis introduced a discordant note in his speech as Shadow Defence Secretary, with: 'I am sceptical about Trident renewal... But I am clear that our party has a policy for Trident renewal.' Lewis also, and unnecessarily, over-egged the Labour Party's commitment to NATO with a fairy tale description of the Atlantic Alliance as 'an organisation that springs directly from our values: collectivism, internationalism and the strong defending the weak'. His statement on Trident caused a predictable flurry of media interest, with claims that Lewis had also intended to say he would not seek to change the policy of backing replacement but had been overruled by the leader's office.

The attempted burial of the nuclear disarmament debate didn't play well. 'What's happened to the defence review?' was a recurring refrain up and down the corridors of conference.

Standing room only at a larger than usual CND fringe meeting and a constant flow of visitors to its stand in the exhibition area, for example, were testimony to continued opposition to Trident.

The Corbyn team did signal the need for a new approach to foreign policy. An NEC statement promised to 'put conflict resolution and human rights at the heart of foreign policy... end support for aggressive wars of intervention and... honour our international treaty obligations on nuclear disarmament'. In her speech to conference, Shadow Foreign Secretary Emily Thornberry reiterated that 'a future Labour government will make the success of talks on multilateral nuclear disarmament a test of foreign policy success'.

Corbyn's anti-war stance won broad support, and the acknowledgement in his speech that the refugee crisis was 'fuelled by wars across the Middle East' was greeted by thunderous applause. He reaffirmed his view of 'the disastrous invasion and occupation of Iraq', reiterated his apology for Labour's role in the war, first made when the Chilcot Report was published, and reasserted the NEC position: 'We need a foreign policy based on peace, justice and human rights... and we need to honour our international treaty obligations on nuclear disarmament and encourage others to do the same.'

This is a welcome start, but it's far from enough. The problem lies in the terms in which the Trident debate has been conducted so far. As in the 1980s, Labour's nuclear lobby has sought to obfuscate rational discussion about the utility of Trident replacement by introducing the notion that getting rid of Trident is unpopular, which is intended to draw Labour loyalists on side.

Billy Hayes adroitly summed up the origins of what amounts to an unpopularity myth:

'The lessons of 1983 for Mandelson and the leadership were that you can't win from the left... The left is going against accepted nostrums. Like *The Matrix*,[1] the left is going against what's perceived as reality.'

The claim that nuclear disarmament is unpopular is not only open to challenge. It also serves to avoid two other crucial issues. The first is that of appealing to a section of the electorate that is unlikely to vote Labour regardless of maintaining nuclear weapons. Mandelson's notion of election strategy being the crucial appeal to a mythical middle ground was largely unchallenged – and not only on the nuclear issue – until Corbyn took the leadership. The second is that of constructing a campaign that embeds both the reasons and the need for nuclear disarmament in public consciousness.

Hayes offered two examples of why we can believe that a nuclear disarmament campaign by Labour can and will change:

'The terms of the debate on nuclear weapons hasn't changed much since the 1980s, but the debate on war *has* changed. That's definite. Nowadays it's not seen as controversial to be against intervention; it's much more acceptable to talk about non-interventionism...

'The lesson of the GLC in the 1980s for me was that you can popularise apparently unpopular things. Look at what Livingstone did on anti-racism for example, and he did it again at the GLA in a more muted way. The left has got to be about the future. You can't rely on a vision of the past.'

---

1   *The Matrix* is a cult sci-fi film that depicts a dystopian future in which reality as perceived by most humans is actually simulated by the Matrix, a means developed by sentient machines to subdue the human population so they can be used as an energy source for the machines.

DODGY DEBATE

Britain's nuclear warriors offer three basic reasons for having nuclear weapons. The first is deterrence, which ignores the complexities of international relations in favour of an outdated Cold War view of the world. The second is a faux multilateralism, which disregards Britain's role in proliferation as a nuclear weapons state that intends to upgrade its capability. The pro-nuclear version of multilateralism amounts to making multilateral steps by Britain conditional on everyone else taking them first. In reality, over the years Britain has blocked a number of attempts by the UN to promote multilateral initiatives.

The third argument is that of jobs. Few in the labour and peace movements will argue that we shouldn't take this seriously. Britain's shrinking manufacturing base has meant that the defence industry (as a whole, that is, not just nuclear) now accounts for around one quarter of all British manufacturing. Diversification is an important, but separate, component in the debate about Trident, a debate which cannot start from the implicit assumption that the possession of weapons of mass, indiscriminate destruction is justified by the need to protect skilled employment.

This is ignored by the GMB, which argues the jobs case without reference to the end product of its members 'industrial output'. Unite accepts in abstract the arguments for getting rid of nuclear weapons, but the leadership insists that the government of the day must first guarantee every job before the union is willing to engage in a diversification debate. This ignores the need to discuss with its ally how a future Labour government could protect those workers whose Trident jobs were at risk. In his 2015 leadership campaign Corbyn called for a government-controlled diversification agency, which would have to be part of any overarching industrial strategy elaborated by McDonnell's team. The GMB and Unite have yet to respond to this initiative.

The overriding reason that successive Labour leaderships have defended the possession of nuclear weapons is political rather than military, and rarely spoken about. As the previous chapters have shown, since 1945 this overarching rationale is less to do with the actual threats Britain faces, than government's belief that nuclear weapons uphold Britain's status as a first rank power. Whatever the military justification may or may not have been in the 1940s, Trident is no protection against systemic threats (should they exist) to Britain.

REAL LESSONS FROM 1983

Looking beyond the arguments of those who seek to preserve the nuclear status quo, Ann Black and Walter Wolfgang, like Hayes, also sought to address some real and difficult lessons from Labour's electoral failures of the 1980s. Black argued:

> 'The situation as regards nuclear weapons was completely different in 1983. And although I was actively involved in CND at the time, I could see there were arguments on the other side – you had the Berlin Wall in place, and SS-20s in East Germany. There were arguments for... a stand-off. I didn't agree with them but I don't think they were completely barking...
>
> 'Andy Burnham said in his hustings for the [2010] leadership campaign I want to keep an independent deterrent because I've got young children and I want to make sure I'm safe. An insurance policy means if my house blows up I can get money to build it again and to stay in a hotel while it's being rebuilt; the same goes if my neighbour blows up my house. It doesn't mean I blow up my neighbour's house so we both end up with nowhere to live. That's not an insurance policy.'

Wolfgang took a broader view:

'The only lesson you can draw is that with a major change in policy a conference resolution is not enough. You have to persuade people to agree with it. And so in 1983 Callaghan and other prominent Labour people were able to sabotage nuclear disarmament.

'Other areas of policy have to be made consistent with nuclear disarmament. Even if we carry conference on Trident completely, acceptance by the leadership may be qualified – I don't say it will be, I don't think it should be – and even if it isn't, other policies will be used to modify it.

'Nuclear disarmament needs a foreign policy which is based on the principles of the United Nations Charter... Foreign policy should exclude a military policy which says you have a capacity to interfere anywhere in the world. All you need is a military policy capable of defending these islands. And that means a reduction of military expenditure. But before we've achieved these, the fact that we haven't got them will be used to sabotage anti-nuclear policy.'

SPLITS DON'T WIN ELECTIONS

If Labour is to win the next election, it must take two lessons to heart. The first is a truth universally acknowledged, to borrow from the quintessentially English Jane Austen: political party splits don't win elections. But just like Austen's rich and single man, Labour is sadly in want of such acknowledgement. Not every Corbynista or Progress devotee might appreciate this, a few of the newer additions to Labour's parliamentary benches might even waver, but the idea that Blair, Mandelson and Campbell don't understand that leading a constant barrage of attacks against your own party is the biggest obstacle to Labour winning the next election simply beggars belief.

The only logical extrapolation to be made from their extraordinary behaviour is that New Labour would rather see the party defeated in a general election than lose their hold over the direction of Labour politics; and they are carrying some of the traditional Labour right along with them. We have seen this before – in the Gang of Four's split over nuclear disarmament and Europe in 1981; and in Callaghan's attacks on nuclear disarmament in the 1983 election. Once again, New Labour would forego the ability to form a government in order to uphold their own narrow interpretation of what direction Labour should take Britain in. The scientific term for this dogmatic and intolerant approach is sectarianism.

This is not to argue that Labour will win the election if opposition is stifled. On the contrary, the attempted silencing of opposition within the party in the past three decades saw internal democracy wither and members' enthusiasm fade. But disagreeing doesn't mean running to your mates in the media with this or that juicy morsel of controversy that feeds the Tory agenda and that of the tiny band of media owners. And Tom Watson understands this as much as New Labour does, as his skilful campaign on phone hacking by Murdoch's News International empire demonstrated.

FACING FORWARD

The second election-winning lesson is that Labour must face forward not backward. New Labour's attacks on Corbyn amount to a demand that he return to the old Blair-era order of tail-ending neo-liberalism and reasserting Britain's imperial role. If only Corbyn would drop all this nonsense about getting to grips with austerity and change his mind about the bomb, he'd soon become a jolly decent fellow too. But his break with this dead-end bipartisanship of parliamentary politics is the very reason for Corbyn's unanticipated popularity. New Labour policies might have drawn paeons of praise from the London counting houses and gentlemen's clubs, but they're sure-fire vote losers at the next election. And it's time for Progress to wake up and smell the coffee.

By way of example, contrast Team Corbyn's approach on two issues at the top of voter concerns – the NHS and housing – where New Labour didn't just tolerate private profit, it actively promoted it. Blair's election in 1997 marked the start of a transition away from the NHS as a national, public sector provider. Disguised in the rhetoric of choice, he introduced private provision and began the piecemeal breakup of the health service. One third of NHS England contracts now go to the private sector. Corbyn is committed to ending private provision.

Blair stressed home ownership as the answer to a growing housing crisis. His 2005 manifesto said merely that Labour would 'give local authorities the ability to start building homes again'. Corbyn's pledge to build one million homes, half of them council owned, in the course of a single parliament is not only super-popular, it's economically efficient. Borrowing to build when interest rates are low boosts the construction industry, helps create jobs, and provides the government with a financial return in the form of increased tax revenues and rental income.

New Labour's international role is no less unpopular than its failure to act against market excesses. Indeed, the continuing hostility to Blair's role in the war on Iraq, 13 years after the invasion, is remarkable in itself. Attempting to defend that role, or more recently the decision to air-bomb Syria, simply reminds voters of where delusions of imperial grandeur lead. New Labour squandered billions on unwinnable wars in the Middle East, actions which made things worse not better for the countries under attack, created a refugee crisis on an enormous scale, and helped bring terrorism onto the streets of Britain. Blair's wars squandered billions of government money, and exposed deep dishonesty at the heart of government. This should be acknowledged, as Corbyn does, and Labour should adopt a new, modern foreign policy.

The need for the latter was exposed in a sharp *Question Time* exchange a week before the leadership results were announced. When Alastair Campbell told fellow panellist John

McDonnell 'you and yours are destroying' the Labour Party, McDonnell responded: 'You're the one who created a political environment where no one actually believed a word a politician said. You took us to the edge. We're trying to restore the confidence in politics again that you destroyed... You lost us five million votes in that process and set us up to fail. The reason Jeremy was elected is because people wanted some honesty back in politics again.' We should all take note that McDonnell's remarks drew loud applause from an audience that was far from universally sympathetic to Labour.

TRIDENT'S FORWARD MARCH
Scrapping Trident is an indivisible part of Labour's forward march. The heated debate in Labour's ranks is not reflected in public opinion. Talk to your next door neighbour, your mates in the pub or club, chat to that person sitting on the bus next to you. You'll find little appetite for nuclear weapons. Opinion has changed. Nuclear disarmament is mainstream. The problem is one of 'operationalising' those sentiments, putting pressure on politicians to understand and honour them.

In the 1940s-50s and again in the 1980s, people were conscious of nuclear weapons as a clear and present danger – of their possible use in Korea or Vietnam for example, or in a war in Europe between the United States and the Soviet Union. Fear drove them onto the streets. Nowadays entire generations have become acclimatised to the idea that nuclear weapons exist without being used, so that they are no longer foremost among people's concerns.

The idea of a foreign policy for Britain based on human security, peace and conflict resolution cannot be advanced while this country continues to possess nuclear weapons. Those of us who understand that have an important part to play in persuading the rest of the Labour Party to understand it too.

It's appropriate to end with the words of Walter Wolfgang again, who helped organise the first Ban the Bomb march back in the 1950s. Asked what he would like the next Labour manifesto to say, Wolfgang replied with a concise summary of what many Labour Party members want and believe:

> 'Labour regards the possession and use of nuclear weapons by anybody to be a major threat to human survival. We will pursue a policy aimed at a step by step agreement to achieve global nuclear disarmament. In order to make this possible Labour will discourage nuclear proliferation and abandon the Trident system and any other. Our foreign policy will be based on the principles of the United Nations Charter and will avoid military aggression. The abandonment of nuclear weapons and excessive military expenditure will make our economic objectives easier to achieve.'

APPENDIX 1

The interviews

The interviews, which took place between October and December 2013 are an important element of the research project commissioned by NET, the Nuclear Education Trust, and a core component of this book. The extracts included in *Corbyn and Trident* add colour and atmosphere to the narrative. They bestow a behind-the-scenes flavour of what it was like to be part of the actions and decisions being recounted.

The purpose of the interviews was to record experiences and opinions from different sides of the policy debate within the Labour Party and, to a lesser extent, outside it; so that taken together they would provide an authentic flavour of contemporaneous opinion. Each interview is a first-hand account by an expert witness who helped shape the course of the events they describe. Many of the interviewees contributed in significant ways to Labour's policy formation, but no longer play the roles described in their interviews. So setting down their narratives was timely and urgent.

Each question set was tailored to the particular experiences of the individual informant but, as far as possible, questions covered the same area in most if not all cases. The interviews were semi-structured, and each lasted at least an hour. Participants were encouraged to answer at length and asked to give examples from their own experiences wherever possible. They were provided with open-ended questions in advance of the interview, and warned that follow-up questions arising from their answers might be introduced during the interview.

The questions were trialled in advance to highlight any problems with the way in which they were formulated (for example, leading questions rather than open-ended) and to uncover any pertinent areas that might be missing from the question set. Those trialling were chosen for their understanding of research procedures and/or knowledge of the subject matter, but were not and had not been involved in or able to influence the events under consideration. Those trialling were, of course, required to maintain confidentiality.

With the participant's permission, the interview was voice recorded. Each interviewee was provided with a copy of the voice recording and a transcript of the interview, and given the opportunity to accept or redact their comments. They were offered the choice of being named or remaining anonymous. Each interviewee was provided with my brief description of who they were and what they represented, and invited to amend the description. Everyone interviewed agreed to be named. No interviewee redacted any comments, but a small number of minor amendments were made and accepted for clarification.

PARTICIPANTS

The participants are listed below in alphabetical order:

Rodney Bickerstaffe, former General Secretary, National Union of Public Employees, which later became UNISON. The union was an early support of nuclear disarmament.

Ann Black, member, Labour Party National Executive Committee and National Policy Forum since the late 1990s, and co-founder of the Centre Left Grassroots Alliance.

Nick Brown, Labour MP for Newcastle upon Tyne East since 1983, held ministerial offices in the Blair government and was Labour chief or deputy chief whip under Blair and Brown; a supporter of NATO and an opponent of Trident replacement.

Jeremy Corbyn, Labour MP for Islington North since 1983, formerly Chair of Parliamentary CND and Vice-Chair of CND. Elected Labour leader after his interview took place, he is now a Vice-President of CND.

John Edmonds, former General Secretary, GMB, and a member of Labour's National Campaign Committee during the 1980s-90s. GMB members work in the nuclear and defence industries. The union was and remains an opponent of nuclear disarmament.

Billy Hayes, former General Secretary, Communication Workers Union and a leading trade union opponent of Trident replacement.

Bruce Kent, former Chair and General Secretary of CND, a delegate to Labour Party conference in 1989 and an unsuccessful Labour candidate in 1992 general election.

Julian Lewis, Conservative MP for New Forest East since 1997, regarded as a Thatcherite on defence and security policy. He was a Shadow Defence Minister under John Major, and is now Chair of the Defence Select Committee.

Joan Ruddock, Labour MP for Lewisham Deptford from 1987 to 2015, and Minister of State for Energy in the Blair government. She was Labour candidate for Newbury in 1979, co-founder of Newbury Campaign Against Cruise Missiles, and Chair of CND from 1981 to 1985.

Walter Wolfgang, an organiser of the first Aldermaston march, now Chair of Labour CND and a Vice-President of CND. He has been a Labour Party member since 1948, and served as a constituency party representative on the Labour NEC from 2006 to 2008.

APPENDIX 2
Selected bibliography

POST-WAR BRITISH HISTORY
Tony Benn, *Arguments for democracy*, Jonathan Cape, 1981
Alec Cairncross, *Years of recovery: British economic policy 1945-51*, Methuen, 1985
Stuart Hall and Martin Jacques, *The politics of Thatcherism*, Lawrence and Wishart, 1983
Peter Hennessey, *Never again: Britain 1945-1951*, Vintage, 1993
Peter Hennessey, *Distilling the frenzy: writing the history of one's own times*, Biteback, 2003
Ben Jackson and Robert Saunders (eds), *Making Thatcher's Britain*, Cambridge University Press, 2012
Ronald Reagan's address to the British parliament, 8 June 1982, *The History Place*, Great Speeches Collection
Shirley Williams et al, 'Limehouse Declaration', 25 January 1981, Liberal History website

LABOUR PARTY
CR Attlee, *The Labour Party in perspective*, Victor Gollancz, 1937
Aneurin Bevan, *In place of fear*, Quartet Books, 1990
Terrence Casey, *The Blair legacy*, Palgrave Macmillan, 2009
David Coates, *Prolonged labour: the slow birth of new Labour Britain*, Palgrave Macmillan, 2005
Grace Crookall-Greening and Rosalie Huzzard, *Labouring for peace*, CAM Yorkshire, 2011
Geoffrey Foote, *The Labour Party's political thought: a history*, 2nd edition, Croom Helm, 1985

Graham Goodlad, 'Attlee, Bevin and Britain's Cold War', *History Review* 69, 2011

Patrick Gordon-Walker, *The cabinet*, Jonathan Cape, 1972

Peter Jones, *America and the British Labour Party: the special relationship at work*, Tauris, 1997

John Kampfner, *Blair's wars*, Free Press, 2003

Peter Mandelson, *The Blair revolution revisited*, Politicos, 2002

Lewis Minkin, *The contentious alliance: trade unions and the Labour Party*, Edinburgh University Press, 1991

Kenneth O Morgan, *Labour in power: 1945-1951*, Oxford University Press, 1985

Ben Pimlott and Chris Cook (eds), *Trade unions in British politics: the first 250 years*, 2nd edition, Longman, 1991

David Rubinstein, *The Labour Party and British society 1880-2005*, Sussex Academic Press, 2006

Len Scott, 'Labour and the bomb: the first 80 years', *International Affairs*, 22 June 2006

Len Scott, 'Selling or selling out nuclear disarmament? Labour, the Bomb, and the 1987 General Election', *International History Review*, 2 February 2012

Eric Shaw, *The Labour Party since 1945*, Blackwell, 1996

Andrew Thorpe, *A history of the British Labour Party*, 3rd edition, Palgrave Macmillan, 2008

NATO, NUCLEAR WEAPONS, US POLICY

Gar Alperovitz, *Atomic diplomacy: Hiroshima to Potsdam*, Penguin, 1985

Stephen Ambrose, *Rise to globalism: American foreign policy since 1938*, Penguin, 1985

Atomic Bomb Museum, www.atomicbombmuseum.org

Ian Davis, 'The British bomb and NATO: six decades of "contributing" to NATO's strategic nuclear deterrent', *Sipri*, November 2015

Lawrence Freedman, *The evolution of nuclear strategy*, 3rd edition, Palgrave Macmillan, 2003

Fred Halliday, *The making of the second Cold War*, Verso 1983

John Hersey, *Hiroshima*, Penguin Modern Classics, 1986

Hibakusha Stories, UN-affiliated NGO at http://www.hibakusha stories.org

Michael J Hogan (ed), *The end of the Cold War: its meaning and implications*, Cambridge University Press, 1992

David Holloway, *Stalin and the bomb: the Soviet Union and atomic energy 1939-1956*, Yale University Press, 1994

Diana Johnson, *The politics of Euromissiles*, Verso, 1984

Lawrence S Kaplan, *The United States and Nato: the formative years*, University Press of Kentucky, 1984

John J Mearsheimer, 'Back to the future: instability in Europe after the Cold War', *International Security*, vol 15 no 1, 1990

Joseph Smith (ed), *The origins of Nato*, University of Exeter Press, 1990

The Nuclear Weapon Archive at http://nuclearweaponarchive.org

Tribune, 'Labour and the H-Bomb', 20 September 1957

Voice of Hibakusha at www.inicom.com/hibakusha

BIOGRAPHIES

Michael Foot, *Aneurin Bevan*, Vols I, II, Four Square, 1966

Denis Healey, *The time of my life*, Penguin, 1989

Kevin Jefferys (ed), *Labour forces from Ernest Bevin to Gordon Brown*, IB Tauris, 2002

Kevin Jefferys, *Leading Labour: from Keir Hardie to Tony Blair*, IB Tauris, 1999

RW Johnson, 'Already a member', *London Review of Books*, 36:17, September 2014 (review of Michael Jago's *Clement Attlee: the inevitable prime minister*, Biteback, 2013)

Kenneth O Morgan, *Labour people: leaders and lieutenants, Hardie to Kinnock*, Oxford University Press, 1989

Fritz Stern, 'Ernest Bevin: foreign secretary', in *Foreign Affairs*, vol 62, no 5, Summer 1984

PEACE MOVEMENT

April Carter, *Peace movements: international protest and world politics since 1945*, Routledge, 2014

Channel 4 TV, 'MI5's Official Secrets' documentary, *20/20 Vision*, March 1985

Conservative and Unionist Central Office, *Labour's CND cover-up: the doctored files of Labour candidates*, April 1992

Kate Hudson, *CND: now more than ever*, Vision Paperbacks, 2005

John Minnion and Philip Bolsover (eds), *The CND story*, Allison and Busby, 1983

Ann Pettitt, *Walking to Greenham: how the peace camp began and the Cold War ended*, Honno, 2006

United Nations Office for Disarmament Affairs (UNODA), at https://www.un.org/disarmament

PUBLIC OPINION

David Capitanchik and Richard C Eichenberg, 'Defence and public opinion', *Chatham House Paper No 20*, Routledge, 1983

Connie De Boer, 'The polls: the European peace movement and deployment of nuclear missiles', in *Public Opinion Quarterly*, Spring 85, vol. 49 issue 1

Marco Giugni (ed), *Social protest and policy change: ecology, anti-nuclear and peace movements*, Rowman and Littlefield, 2004

Thomas W Graham and Bernard M Kramer, 'The polls: ABM and star wars, attitudes towards nuclear defense, 1945-1985', *Public Opinion Quarterly*, Spring 86, vol 50 issue 1

Catherine Marsh and Colin Fraser (eds), *Public opinion and nuclear weapons*, Macmillan, 1989

Mildred Strunk, *Public Opinion 1935-1946*, Princeton University Press, 1951

CONTEMPORARY AND NEWS SOURCES

Ann Black, NEC reports, at http://www.clga.org.uk

Campaign for Labour Party Democracy, at http://www.clpd.org.uk

Campaign for Nuclear Disarmament, at http://www.cnduk.org

Centre Left Grassroots Alliance, at http://grassrootslabour.net and http://www.clga.org.uk

General election results, *UK political info*, http://www.ukpolitical.info

Hansard, official parliament records, at https://hansard.parliament.uk

House of Commons Library publications, at http://www.parliament.uk/business/publications/research

Ipsos Mori, at https://www.ipsos-mori.com

Labour Briefing, at http://labourbriefing.squarespace.com/home

Labour CND, at http://www.labourcnd.org.uk

Labour Left Briefing (also known as *Original Briefing*), at http://www.labourbriefing.co.uk

Labour List, at http://labourlist.org

Labour Party, www.labour.org.uk

Labour Representation Committee (LRC), at http://l-r-c.org.uk

Left Futures, at http://www.leftfutures.org

Margaret Thatcher Foundation, at www.margaretthatcher.org

Momentum, at http://www.peoplesmomentum.com

Political party manifestos, at http://www.politicsresources.net

Progress, at http://www.progressonline.org.uk

YouGov, at https://yougov.co.uk

Charley Allan, 'Saving Labour one dirty trick at a time', *Morning Star*, 18 July 2016

BBC News online, 'Labour leadership: Jeremy Corbyn completes the line-up', 15 June 2015

Owen Bowcott, 'UK discussed plans to help mujahideen weeks after Soviet invasion of Afghanistan', *Guardian*, 30 December 2010

Matt Chorley, 'Labour could face four election defeats: Blair warns of disaster if party lurches to the left under leadership frontrunner Corbyn', *Daily Mail,* 23 July 2015

Daily Telegraph, Field Marshal Lord Carver Obituary, 11 December 2001

Ben Glaze, 'Labour leadership race: Jeremy Corbyn could win by a knockout under new voting procedure', *Daily Mirror*, 11 August 2015

Guardian video, 'BBC's Laura Kuenssberg hissed at as she questions Jeremy Corbyn', 2 June 2016

Alex Holland, 'Is Trident New Labour's shibboleth?', *New Statesman*, 10 September 2010

Solomon Hughes, 'With friends like this Labour hardly needs enemies', *Morning Star*, 6 September 2016

LabourList, 'Corbyn to set out 10-point plan to "transform Britain" ahead of first leadership debate', 4 August 2016

Richard Littlejohn, 'I'm a politician...get me out of here', *Daily Mail*, 19 August 2016

Nyta Mann, 'Foot's message of hope to left', BBC News online, 14 July 2003

Paul Mason, 'The sound of Blairite silence', Medium.com, 18 August 2016

Thatcher Reagan explosive love story poster, https://www.flickr.com/photos/dullhunk/7115239689

James Wright, 'The paper trail that proves once and for all where Owen Smith's allegiances lie', *The Canary*, 21 September 2016

Patrick Wintour, 'Jeremy Corbyn: I would never use nuclear weapons if I were PM', *Guardian*, 30 September 2015

Adam Withnall, 'Former Blair advisor says NEC decision to allow Corbyn on ballot "has killed the Labour party"', *Independent*, 12 July 2016

Liam Young, 'Owen Smith's comments on Isis are totally different to Corbyn's stance on the IRA', iNews, 17 August 2016